Batter their Walls, Gates and Forts

The Proceedings of the 2022 English Civil War Fortress Symposium

Edited by Stephen Ede-Borrett & David Flintham

'This is the Century of the Soldier', Fulvio Testi, Poet, 1641

Helion & Company Limited
Unit 8 Amherst Business Centre
Budbrooke Road
Warwick
CV34 5WE
England
Tel. 01926 499 619
Email: info@helion.co.uk
Website: www.helion.co.uk
Twitter: @helionbooks
Visit our blog http://blog.helion.co.uk/

Published by Helion & Company 2023
Designed and typeset by Mary Woolley (www.battlefield-design.co.uk)
Cover designed by Paul Hewitt, Battlefield Design (www.battlefield-design.co.uk)

Text © as individually credited 2023
Illustrations as individually credited

Every reasonable effort has been made to trace copyright holders and to obtain their permission for the use of copyright material. The author and publisher apologize for any errors or omissions in this work and would be grateful if notified of any corrections that should be incorporated in future reprints or editions of this book.

ISBN 978-1-804514-61-0

British Library Cataloguing-in-Publication Data.
A catalogue record for this book is available from the British Library.

All rights reserved. No part of this publication may be reproduced, stored in a retrieval system, or transmitted, in any form, or by any means, electronic, mechanical, photocopying, recording or otherwise, without the express written consent of Helion & Company Limited.

For details of other military history titles published by Helion & Company Limited contact the above address or visit our website: http://www.helion.co.uk.

We always welcome receiving book proposals from prospective authors.

Contents

List of Contributors	iv
English Civil War Fortresses Symposium – Proceedings: Foreword from the Fortress Study Group	vi
English Civil War Fortresses Symposium – Proceedings: Introduction from the Battlefields Trust	viii
A Tale of Two Cities: Garrisons, Strongholds, Fortifications and Sieges in the English Civil War by Peter Gaunt	9
The Siege of Moreton Corbet Castle: A case study of the archaeological evidence of attack and defence at a small garrison siege of the War of the Three Kingdoms by Richard Leese	41
King's Lynn Under Siege: How a small field in North Lynn is changing our understanding of English Civil War fortress engineering by David Flintham	63
Newark in the Civil Wars by Kevin Winter	88
A Small Fort in Devon: How Forty Musketeers Changed History by Nick Arnold	105
The Civil War Defences and Siegeworks of Oxford by David Radford	139

List of Contributors

Professor Peter Gaunt

During the 1980s Peter Gaunt held a succession of mainly non-academic posts, including work on a range of archaeological excavations and surveys, as an architectural historian for English Heritage (working mainly on Hampton Court Palace) and as a researcher/writer for the parks and palaces division of the Department of the Environment (working mainly on the Tower of London and Kensington Palace and Gardens). Professor Gaunt also undertook a range of free-lance commissions, including work on guide books, on picture research and captioning, and on a number of exhibitions and interpretative strategies.

Although in the main Professor Gaunt was working outside academia at this stage, he continued to research and write and to have scholarly material published. This process was aided by a year spent living and working at Wellington in New Zealand in the mid 1980s as a post-doctoral fellow of the Victoria University of Wellington. He returned full time to academic work in the late 1980s and since then has held teaching posts at the University of Wales (Swansea), the University of London (Royal Holloway) and the University of Chester.

His interests range over history and archaeology, especially visiting castles, churches and chapels. He also enjoys second-hand bookshops and acquiring (he says 'too many') second hand books, walking and photography.

Dr Richard Leese

Dr Richard Leese is researcher studying the archaeology of early modern sieges of the Wars of the Three Kingdoms in England. Richard completed his doctoral studies in 2022 at the University of Huddersfield under the supervision of Dr Glenn Foard. Prior to doctoral research, Richard studied Battlefield and Conflict Archaeology at the University of Glasgow in 2012–2013, and is a War Studies graduate of the University of Wolverhampton. His current research interests include examining bullet impact scars on structures, metal detector survey strategies of fields of conflict from the Wars of the Three Kingdoms, and the archaeology of civil defence preparation during the Cold War.

David Flintham

David Flintham is the co-founder and project director of the King's Lynn under Siege community archaeology project. He is the author of three books (with a fourth due for publication by Helion in 2023), and more than 60 other papers, essays and articles on mid-seventeenth century fortress warfare, particularly across the British Isles. David is also part of a research project 're-discovering' London's English Civil War fortifications. A long-time member of the Fortress Study Group, he now serves on its committee. He has also been a member of the Battlefields Trust for a number of years.

Kevin Winter

After 34 years in the Royal Navy, and looking for a new challenge when he retired at the age of 50. Kevin Winter began to look at a second career in the museum sector after volunteering at the National Museum of the Royal Navy in Portsmouth during his final two years' service. He applied for a job as Museum Assistant with Newark & Sherwood Museum Service and began work there in December 2009. After a variety of different roles in collections and learning he is currently the Collections and Exhibitions Officer at the National Civil War Centre, Newark Museum.

Some 11 years ago he was recruited into the Battlefields Trust and became Chair of the East Midlands Region. In 2018 he successfully fundraised for the installation of interpretation panels for the Battle of Stoke Field (1487). Additionally he is also involved in a number of local, and national, heritage organisations.

Nick Arnold

Although best-known as the author of the 'Horrible Science' children's book series, Nick Arnold trained as a historian. He read History at York and wrote his research degree thesis on the history of newspapers. He has had a life-long interest in military history, fortifications, and archaeology, and in recent years has published papers on the probable locations of the Battle of Cynuit (878) and the Battle of Northam (1069). In 2006 Nick Arnold was the founder and first Director of the Appledore Book Festival.

David Radford

David Radford has been the City Council Archaeologist at Oxford since 2008 and has worked in the field for over 30 years

English Civil War Fortresses Symposium – Proceedings

Foreword from the Fortress Study Group

Formed in 1975, the Fortress Study Group is a charity devoted to the study and preservation of fortifications in the age of artillery (roughly from 1500), and aims 'To advance the education of the public in the study of all aspects of fortifications and their armaments, especially works constructed to mount or resist artillery.'

The Civil Wars of the mid-seventeenth century were a pivotal point in the development of artillery fortification across the British Isles: the wars marked the swansong of the medieval castle, as well as being the first major 'test' of the purpose-built artillery forts constructed during the Tudor period. They also demonstrated that the country house could, on occasion, be surprisingly resistant to attack. Towns and cities throughout the country were fortified, while the citadels constructed during the 1650s, the ultimate example of Civil War fortification, set the standard for British fortification for the next hundred years.

However, it was the earthwork fortification that came to typify the Civil Wars: these were relatively quick to build, but as a result, they disappeared almost as easily, with the consequence that despite once covering virtually every corner of England, Ireland, Scotland, and Wales, they are now a largely forgotten aspect of the military history of the British Isles.

Both contemporaries and recent scholars have demonstrated that fortress warfare was the prevailing form of action during the Civil Wars. Roger Boyle, 1st Earl of Orrery, a veteran of the fighting in Ireland, commented that, 'we make war more like foxes than lions, and you will have twenty sieges for one battle.'[1] More recently, the late Christopher Duffy described the conflict as 'a war of trenches, ramparts, palisades, bombardments and blockades.' Glenn Foard and Richard Morris identified 242 sieges in England during the Wars, and as some places were besieged more than once, equating to 189 major siege sites. This compares with

---

1 Roger Boyle, Earl of Orrery, *A Treatise on the Art of War*, (London, 1677), p.15

30 major battles in England between 1640 and 1651.[2] As not every place that was fortified during the wars was actually besieged, the actual number of fortresses is considerably greater. But despite this, the study of Civil War fortification is still something of the poor relation in the military histories of the period.

Yet, there are a number of research and archaeological projects up and down the country investigating both fortresses and sieges, and the Fortress Study Group, along with the Battlefields Trust, was delighted to bring several of these together in November 2022 at the *English Civil War Fortress Symposium*, the first ever event of its kind, which took place in Newark-upon-Trent, a town rightly renowned for its extant Civil War fortifications. The presenters were acknowledged experts in their respective fields, and the topics ranged from major urban fortifications to minor siege sites, and included fascinating insights on reading musket-ball scars on masonry, and how earthwork ramparts were constructed.

The Fortress Study Group is equally pleased that the papers presented at the symposium are published here, a book that is sure to be welcomed by students, both of the Civil Wars, and the development of British artillery fortifications.

The symposium has provided new impetus for the study of fortifications and sieges during the Civil Wars, and the Fortress Study Group looks forward to presenting future research in its annual peer reviewed Journal (*FORT*) and in its *CASEMATE* Magazine. For further information about the FSG, including membership, visit https://www.fortressstudygroup.org.

David Flintham
(On behalf of the Fortress Study Group)
August 2023

---

[2] Glenn Foard and Richard Morris, *Archaeology of English Battlefields*, (York: Council for British Archaeology, 2012), pp.127, 175–9.

English Civil War Fortresses Symposium – Proceedings

Introduction from the Battlefields Trust

As the national heritage organisation devoted to the preservation, research and presentation of battlefields as historical and educational resources, the Battlefields Trust's joint sponsorship of the 2022 *English Civil War Fortress symposium* with the Fortress Study Group might appear to some to go slightly beyond its remit.

But many Civil War fortifications were besieged, stormed or otherwise attacked and the area around fortifications, the 'siegefield', was often very much a battlefield. Moreover, the course of the war, and therefore the context in which its battles were fought, cannot be understood without an understanding of the nature and importance of defended places and the fortifications that surrounded them.

With this in mind, the Battlefields Trust was keen to support the first national symposium looking at these issues and we were not disappointed. All the presentations offered insight into the nature of Civil War defences and their importance with many directly highlighting the fighting that occurred across their ditches, bastions and curtain walls.

The Battlefields Trust therefore commends the proceedings of the symposium to you and would like to record its thanks to the contributors, Professor Peter Gaunt, Richard Leese, David Flintham, Kevin Winter, Nick Arnold, Rachel Askew and David Radford. A particular thanks goes to David Flintham from the Fortress Study Group who did much of the heavy lifting in organising the symposium.

For further information about the Battlefields Trust, including how to join and help it preserve Britain's battlefields see www.battlefieldstrust.com.

Simon Marsh
Battlefields Trust Research and Threats Coordinator
August 2023

A Tale of Two Cities

Garrisons, Strongholds, Fortifications and Sieges in the English Civil War[1]

Peter Gaunt

> [T]his present unhappy Civill Warre sets its severall Counties in unwonted postures, and renders them in various shapes to all beholders; now quiet, anon troubled; yesterday in plenty, to day in want; every day in feare, and no day under security ... Warre is a wombe big with many miseries, when it travels; it swels envy, quickens malice, begets jealousies, separates friends, undoes families and Kingdomes; its anger is fierce, wrath cruell, instruments of cruelty are in its habitations ... [it] fills the eyes with miserable spectacles, and loads the ears with sad relations... [2]

---

1   As well as the lecture from which this chapter springs, delivered at the English Civil War Fortress symposium held at Newark in November 2022, a version of the material found in the second half of this chapter, on Gloucester and Chester, was given at a day-conference organised by University Centre Shrewsbury in conjunction with Helion Press held in Shrewsbury in November 2019. The author is most grateful for all the comments and questions received from the audiences on both occasions. The material has been revised and slightly expanded for publication, but it consciously retains much of the rhythm and some of the idioms and colloquialisms of an oral presentation; it has been lightly rather than heavily annotated, in the main to give reference to quoted matter and to point readers towards the principal primary and secondary sources upon which the text rests and which provide further information for those who wish to follow up points discussed here.
2   *A True Relation of the Late Victory Obtained by the Right Honourable the Earle of Stanford at Plimmouth and Modbury the 21th of February 1643* (London, 1643), p.2; Thomason acquired his copy on 3 March.

The anonymous author of this pamphlet pulled no punches in terrifying his readers with his relation of the dire effects of civil war. Written and published in the opening weeks of 1643, the first full year of the war, it was in part therefore a prediction more than an account of past events, but its predictions were largely realised in England and Wales over the following three-and-a-half years, down to the conclusion of the main civil war in summer 1646, and again in the briefer, more sporadic but often bitter and sometimes hellish fighting of the so-called second civil war of 1648. That the English and Welsh civil war was indeed a womb big with many miseries has been the thrust and underlying conclusion of much recent work on the wars of the 1640s.[3]

In recent years we have moved away from an approach to the military history of the civil war which not only began, but effectively ended, in focusing just about all attention on a small clutch of military leaders and generals, on the movements and campaigns of their large national armies and on not much more than a handful of large battles, decisive or otherwise. We are now much more in tune with the other side of the war, perhaps the more important aspect given that the majority of troops in England and Wales were caught up in this other type of warfare and fighting during most of the main war of 1642–1646 and that the majority of casualties and fatalities occurred in this aspect of the war. This is the local or county war, a war of small local forces raiding and counter-raiding, bumping into each other unawares or deliberately seeking each other out, a war fought at grass roots level by bodies of troops often a few hundred – or perhaps just a few dozen – strong, a war predicated on the need to tie down, control and suck the resources from the urban and rural environment of England and Wales, a territorial war of scores of small and occasionally larger garrisons based in refortified towns, hastily repaired medieval castles, the odd late medieval or Tudor manor house, the occasional parish church and a scattering of newly built stand alone earthen artillery forts.[4]

---

[3] See, for example, Malcolm Wanklyn and Frank Jones, *The Military History of the English Civil War* (Harlow: Longman, 2004), Barbara Donagan, *War in England, 1642–49* (Oxford: Oxford UP, 2008), Michael Braddick, *God's Fury, England's Fire* (London: Allen Lane, 2008) and Peter Gaunt, *The English Civil War: A Military History* (London: Tauris, 2014).

[4] This type of warfare and war effort have been and is best explored through regional or county studies, for which see, for example, recent works by Jeremy Knight, *Civil War and Restoration in Monmouthshire* (Woonton: Logaston, 2005), Stephen Bull, '*A General Plague of Madness*': *The Civil Wars in Lancashire* (Lancaster: Carnegie, 2009), Malcolm Gratton, *The Parliamentarian and Royalist War Effort in Lancashire, 1642–1651* (Manchester: Chetham Society, 2010), David Ross, *Royalist But…Herefordshire in the English Civil War, 1640-1651* (Woonton: Logaston, 2012), Ian Beckett, *Wanton Troopers: Buckinghamshire in the Civil Wars* (Barnsley: Pen & Sword, 2015) and Jonathan Worton, *To Settle the Crown: Waging Civil War in Shropshire* (Solihull: Helion, 2016).

The civil war had had this side to it right from the outset. Even before the King had raised his standard at Nottingham on 22 August 1642, clashes had occurred, or had begun, for control of a few key urban or semi-rural strongholds. For example, Kingston upon Hull was besieged by the Earl of Lindsey for the King during July but was successfully retained for Parliament by John Hotham and his 1,000 strong garrison secure behind their hastily repaired and upgraded defences. Again, Portsmouth had come out for the King in July under its governor George Goring, but was sealed up and effectively besieged by Sir William Waller in a fairly large-scale military operation in mid-August, involving the use of artillery, leading in due course to its surrender to Parliament in early September. More such operations swiftly followed, such as the successful defence of Manchester by a 1,000 strong Parliamentarian force against the attempts by the Earl of Derby to take it for the King by siege, bombardment and storm in late September. The Marquess of Hertford's attempts to hold the town and castle of Sherborne in Dorset for the King in early September employing a fledgling army at least 3,000 strong failed when they were forced out in quite a substantial military operation by the Earl of Bedford's Parliamentarian force numbering up to 7,000 men, entailing a bitter fight around hedges and walls and in the streets to regain the town, followed by bombardment and counter-bombardment as the Royalists sought to dig in at the castle, only to be forced out from there too.[5]

So at a local level a territorial war of garrisoning key strongholds and of siege, bombardment and storm was already getting underway, even before the Edgehill campaign proper really began. It was, moreover, gathering pace and spreading even as the battle of Edgehill itself was looming. Neither the King nor the Earl of Essex arrived at Edgehill in late October with the full body of troops they had raised to date, for both had taken the decision to devote some of their military manpower to securing and holding key urban and semi-rural strongholds in the region, including Warwick, Coventry and Banbury Castle.

Had either side scored an overwhelming and crushing victory on the plain below the Edgehill escarpment on 23 October, it is possible, perhaps likely, that the conflict would have ended there and that the more local, territorial and garrison-type warfare which was already unfolding would have led nowhere and quickly fizzled out. However, the indecisive nature of the battle and the wider campaign of Edgehill ensured a longer and continuing civil war, and with it the continuation and intensification of the process, already started in key locations

---

5 While not exactly ignored or overlooked, these early clashes tend to be underplayed and accorded little attention in many single-volume military histories of the civil war, which is unfortunate, for in some ways they set the tone for the much more extensive warfare which unfolded in the wake of the Edgehill campaign. See Gaunt, *The English Civil War*, chapter 2.

Sir John Hotham portrayed as a Parliamentarian hero for his defence of Hull in 1642, part of the defences of which are shown behind his rearing horse. He later flirted with royalism, probably intrigued to betray the town and was removed, tried and executed by Parliament. (Public domain).

and regions, of carving up the country and of securing urban and rural territory through fortified strongholds and garrisons placed within them. The territorial war and everything it brought with it – the sort of sites and the issues involving them explored in this volume – was underway and would play a, perhaps *the*, key role in the unfolding conflict.

The distribution of sites fortified and garrisoned in the course of the civil war, and of the resulting military operations against them, was by no means uniform across England and Wales. The pattern and density were determined by two key factors. First, they can be mapped onto the value of the landscape and the environment at a time of civil war. Fortified and garrisoned strongholds were needed to tie down and control strategically valuable territory, such as key rivers and river valleys, bridges and fording points, main roads and road junctions, ports and centres of the production of things like iron, lead, gunpowder and other armaments valuable in wartime. More broadly, they were needed to tie down and control territories rich in the key resources needed to supply and sustain a lengthy war, such as people, horses, fodder, victuals and money, in order to ensure that those resources could be creamed off on a regular basis to keep the Royalist or Parliamentarian war effort going. Thus towns, both as centres of population and as established markets, ports and the richer and more productive agricultural regions were valuable to both sides in the civil war. It was in these strategically important or resource-rich areas where wartime garrisoned strongholds, urban and rural, tended to cluster and to be thick on the ground. Conversely, there was little value in holding or contesting thinly-populated and poor upland areas, where rough grazing and a few scraggy sheep predominated, areas of scattered farmsteads and a few hamlets but of no towns or even villages of any size, crossed by a handful of drovers' roads leading nowhere valuable. Thus much of the interior of Wales and the uplands and mountains at its heart, the Lake District and the Pennine spine, apart from key east–west crossing routes and a few areas rich in metal ore, were of almost no value to either side in the civil war and, with very few exceptions, were not regions of garrisoned towns or refortified medieval castles. They simply were not worth holding and contesting.[6]

---

6   This can be demonstrated very clearly and strikingly by plotting onto a contour map of Wales the towns, castles, manor houses and so on which were fortified and garrisoned by either side during the course of the civil war. With hardly any exceptions – a couple of small and quite short-lived Royalist garrisons in upland Radnorshire – they are absent from land over 200 metres and instead are all clustered around the coasts, in the agriculturally richer and more urbanised parts of South-East Monmouthshire, the Vale of Glamorgan, south Carmarthenshire, South and Mid-Pembrokeshire, Eastern Denbighshire and Flintshire and along the Severn valley as it flows out of Wales and into Shropshire. See Gaunt, *The English Civil War*, map 1.

The second key factor determining the location and density of fortified strongholds on the ground was the degree to which territory was being contested and was vulnerable to attack. The Parliamentarian heartlands of East Anglia and the South-East were generally secure and uncontested during the main war of 1642–1646, sheltered from the front line of the fighting and pretty well immune from the danger of serious or sustained attack by Royalist forces. Accordingly, there was no need to plant garrisons thickly in these 'safe' areas and it would have been a waste of manpower to devote many troops to garrison duties there. There were Parliamentarian garrisons scattered around Norfolk, Suffolk, Essex, Kent, Surrey and Sussex, but they were quite thin on the ground and served more as administrative centres and bases for the collection and gathering of resources than as active fighting strongholds. The same was true for much of the war of Royalist held Cornwall – although Parliament's retention of Plymouth, just over the Tamar estuary, always posed a potential threat – until the last months of the war and, with the rider that in any case much of the interior was of little value, of Royalist control of almost the whole of Wales until the latter stages of the conflict. On the other hand, counties which were divided and disputed, along or close to a contested and often fluid and moving, although sometimes more entrenched and static, frontier between Royalist controlled and Parliamentarian controlled territory, were the areas which were thickly planted with fortified and garrisoned strongholds and where the local war was hottest and fiercest. Thus counties which were divided and disputed for much, or most, of the war, such as Shropshire and Staffordshire in the West Midlands and Nottinghamshire and Lincolnshire in the East Midlands, were thickly planted with garrisoned strongpoints. Again, a map of wartime Wales is instructive: Pembrokeshire was the only part of the Principality which was divided and hotly contested for most of the conflict, with the fortunes of war flowing one way and the other until Parliament finally secured control in 1645–46. There were more fortified and garrisoned towns, castles, manor houses and churches in wartime Pembrokeshire than there were in the whole of the rest of the Wales.[7]

A range of different types and sizes of locations and buildings were fortified and held in the course of the civil war, as reflected in the specific and varied case studies explored in this volume.[8] Most obvious, and probably most numerous, are

---

7 Again, see Gaunt, *The English Civil War*, map 1, though that map somewhat underplays the number of, sometimes small and quite short-lived, garrisons found in Pembrokeshire in the course of the civil war, as there were too many there to squeeze all of them onto a map at that scale.
8 For more about the individual sties and buildings discussed in this and succeeding paragraphs, as well as scores of others, see P. Gaunt, *The Cromwellian Gazetteer* (Stroud: Alan Sutton, 1986). Many also feature in Peter Harrington's trio of studies, *Archaeology*

the scores of towns and urban centres which were fortified and garrisoned across much of England and Wales, two of which will be explored and reassessed in more detail in the second half of this chapter. Repairing existing, generally medieval, urban stone walls, revamping gatehouses and recutting the outer ditches was the norm and was attempted wherever they had survived, but throwing up newly-raised earthwork defences, often termed 'mud walls' in contemporary accounts, was a perfectly effective and viable alternative to encompass and defend towns which either had never possessed medieval stone defences or where they had largely or wholly gone by the mid-seventeenth century. For example, Newport Pagnell, Nantwich and Lyme Regis were fortified and defended in this way during the civil war, the first serving as a Parliamentarian 'super garrison' for much of the war, the other two enduring and surviving close siege in 1644.

Dozens of medieval stone castles were refortified, generally by reroofing and reflooring some or all of the main buildings, adding new outer doors and gates, often with new drawbridge arrangements, often too throwing up fresh outer earthworks to guard the approaches to the re-edified castle or to protect vulnerable faces. Early medieval earthwork and timber castles do not seem to have been refortified and employed during the civil war, even though substantial earthworks with clear military potential, such as raised mottes and circuits of bank and ditch, survived at many of those sites. Equally, some medieval stone castles were clearly too ruinous by the 1640s to be usefully brought back to life in this way, even in contested areas where the two sides were looking to plant numerous garrisons. For example, although in divided and contested Shropshire a dozen or more medieval stone castles were refortified and played some part in the civil war, other stone castles in the county, such as Acton Burnell, Alberbury, Knockin and Whittington, were ignored, probably in the main because they were too far gone to be of use. It is noticeable, too, that although they played a role, housing soldiers, as a magazine, as a command centre and so on, castles in large towns and standing within the circuit of urban defences tended to play a secondary role and it was the town walls and gates that were the focus of attack and defence, as at Bristol, Chester, Exeter, Oxford and York. Those castles which played a bigger and front line role in the fighting in their own right tended to be those adjoining and overlooking – though often slightly distinct from – smaller towns or those which were semi-rural and with no more than a village nearby, castles like Beeston in Cheshire, Corfe and Sherborne in Dorset, Donnington in Berkshire,

---

of the English Civil War (Princes Risborough: Shire, 1992), *English Civil War Archaeology* (London: Batsford, 2004) and *English Civil War Fortifications* (Oxford: Osprey, 2004).

Pontefract, Scarborough and Skipton in Yorkshire, Raglan in Monmouthshire and Montgomery in Montgomeryshire.

Although fewer in number, a range of less obviously military sites and buildings were made use of in the course of the Civil War, sometimes as quite short-lived or secondary bases. Largely or wholly undefended, medieval, Tudor or early Stuart, manor houses – ranging from small and pokey to some of the grandest Jacobean and Elizabethan houses, were fortified, despite the obvious limitations of their undefended entrances and quite large outward facing windows.

In July 1643 Oliver Cromwell cut his teeth besieging, bombarding and successfully storming the grand Elizabethan Burghley House on the borders of Cambridgeshire, into which a Royalist force had fallen back when caught in the open. In autumn 1645, in one of his last independent operations during the main civil war, he besieged, bombarded and successfully stormed mighty Basing House in Hampshire, the huge medieval and Tudor twin houses which had served as a Royalist garrison and a thorn in Parliament's side for much of the war.

Many manor houses in Wiltshire – a County divided and contest in 1643 as the Royalists took control, and again in 1645 as Parliament regained the area – were fortified and garrisoned, perhaps because the County was not particularly well served by surviving medieval stone castles. For example, Great Chalfield House, Lacock House or Abbey (the secular residence had been crafted out of a dissolved abbey) Littlecote House, Longford House and Wilton House, most of them substantially fifteenth or sixteenth century in date, were fortified for King or Parliament at different stages of the war.

On occasion too, churches might serve as temporary bases or as outposts to bigger strongholds, not a sign that either side was irreligious or sacrilegious, but a reflection that in some smaller settlements the church was the only stone building suitable for occupying and mounting a defence. That a church usually came with a lofty stone tower, windows set quite high in the walls, a thick wooden door and in many cases an outer stone or brick wall surrounding the churchyard added to its attraction as at least a short-term bolt hole. In some cases, a church stood so close to the main fortified stronghold that, of necessity and to prevent it serving as a ready-made base for an attacking force, the garrison had to fortify and hold it too as a secondary base. Good examples of this are the churches at Tong and Stokesay in Shropshire, fortified as adjuncts to Tong Castle and to the so-called castle (in reality, more a defended manor house) of Stokesay respectively.

In a handful of cases, new earthworks were thrown up not to defend or to strengthen the environs of a garrisoned town or castle, but to stand alone, by themselves. Very occasionally a transport hub was deemed so important that, even though no existing building or settlement lay at that site, an earthwork, generally in the form of an artillery fort, was constructed and manned to control the

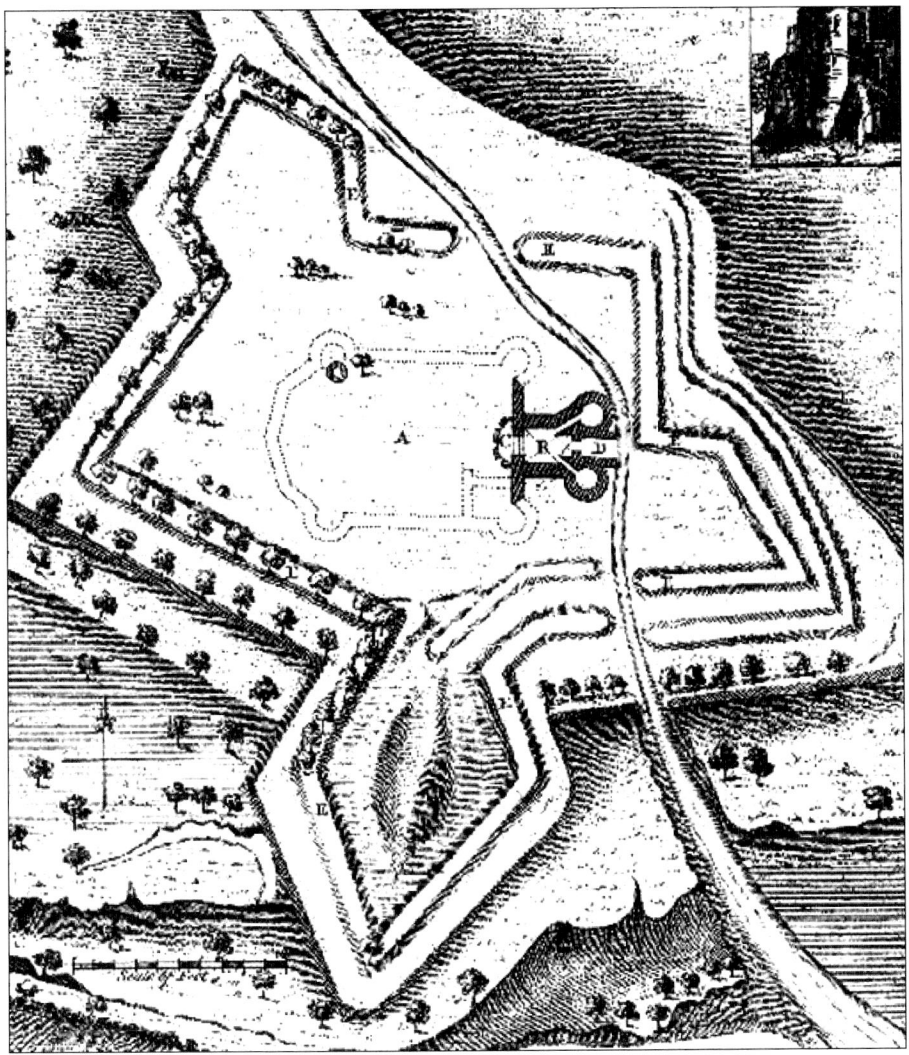

A later print of Donnington Castle, probably dating from the eighteenth century and reproduced in several publications of that and the following century, shows how the castle had been refortified and strengthened by its Royalist garrison during the civil war. The medieval castle had been surrounded and dwarfed by the earthwork banks and ditches of a classic civil war artillery fort, with a number of arrowhead-shaped projecting bastions within which ordinance could be mounted. (Public domain)

immediate vicinity, as with the forts at Earith and Horsey Hill in Cambridgeshire, defending natural or man-made waterways into and through the County.

There are many reasons why we should study civil war fortified sites of this ilk and the military actions which centred upon them. It has already been stressed that strongholds and their garrisons shaped the civil war, in the sense both that they generally determined control of territory at the local level and that they enabled financial and human resources, and much of the other *materiel* of war, to be collected and drawn off and so kept the war and war effort going. In turn, throughout the war both King and Parliament devoted a large proportion of their available manpower to garrison duty and to the local and county war, rather than incorporating them in their main regional or national field armies. More than that, some fortified strongholds and the garrisons they housed were so large, potent and important that they shaped the civil war in the area. Thus for much of the war the Royalists in Cornwall and Devon focussed their efforts on overwhelming the last remaining Parliamentarian stronghold in the region, Plymouth; the conflict in eastern Hampshire was for long periods concentrated on the King's attempt to hold, and Parliament's repeated operations to overwhelm and capture, Basing House; and for almost the entire main civil war the role and threat posed by the Royalist 'super garrison' at Newark on the border of Nottinghamshire and Lincolnshire dominated much of the fighting in that region. Moreover, with good reason contemporaries often felt that attacking and storming a stronghold was the most terrifying and potentially bloodiest type of military operation to be undertaken during the war. Their apprehensions were borne out by the bloodshed and horrors unleashed during and after the successful operations mounted by Prince Rupert to take Birmingham in 1643 and Bolton a year later, the Royalists' capture of Barthomley church in Cheshire at Christmas 1643 and of Hopton Castle in Herefordshire in spring 1644 – Parliamentarians viewed the killings which resulted from these events as massacres – and, whether by accident or design, the deaths of so many within Abbotsbury House in Dorset and Basing House when they fell to Parliament in the autumns of 1644 and 1645 respectively.

We should also be led to these places and to explore these operations by the richness of the surviving source material. Sieges of fortified and garrisoned towns and castles gave rise to some of the most detailed and, from our safe distance, most engaging accounts of military actions during the war. Indeed, they often spawned so-called siege diaries, day-by-day accounts, which are full of human interest and incident of a type provided by few other civil war sources. Detailed contemporary accounts are extant of the sieges of Brampton Bryan Castle, Carlisle, Gloucester, Lathom House, Lyme Regis, Pontefract Castle, Scarborough Castle and Worcester – occasionally from the attackers' viewpoint but more often from the defenders' perspective.⁹ Perhaps even more revealingly, there survive amongst the state papers at the National Archives financial accounts compiled by a good number of Parliamentarian garrisons.¹⁰ Some are rather dry and sparse, and reveal little more than payments of wages to troops of horse, to companies of foot and to individual soldiers and officers. Others, however, are much fuller and from them we can reconstruct something of the day-to-day life of the garrison.

One of the fullest and most detailed surviving sets of garrison accounts, and also one of the most accessible as a full modern transcript is available, provides an insight into the life of the fairly small Parliamentarian garrison at Great Chalfield House during the first half of 1645. The accounts go into great detail about the victuals supplied to, and consumed by, the garrison, for much of the taxes and other levies due to it from the surrounding towns and villages were received in kind rather than in cash. They reveal the delivery of prodigious quantities of pork, bacon, mutton, beef and veal, calves, oxen, bullocks, heifers, steers, pigs and sheep, hens, pullets, capons, turkeys and ducks, beans and peas, wheat, oats, malt and hops, beer, bread, cheese and butter, together with several loads of hay, plus smaller consignments of nutmegs, sugar, cinnamon, fruit and spices, as well as some charcoal. They also record allowances from the taxes due for the care and the diet, including milk, of sick and injured garrison soldiers and for their shrouds when such care failed to save them, as well as for work conducted at or on behalf of the garrison, including carpentry, masonry, sawing, ploughing, haymaking, threshing, tiling, carting, baking and general labouring. From the quantity and variety of food and drink received over this six-month period and bearing in mind

---

9   For Brampton Bryan, see Historical Manuscripts Commission, *The Manuscripts of the Most Honourable the Marquess of Bath, Volume I* (London: HMSO, 1904); for Carlisle, see Isaac Tullie, *A Narrative of the Siege of Carlisle, 1644–45*, Samuel Jefferson (ed.) (Whitehaven: Carlisle Tracts, 1840); for Gloucester, see John Dorney, *A Brief and Exact Relation of the Most Material and Remarkable Passages* (London, 1643); for Lathom House, see Edward Halsall or Edward Chisenhall, *A Journal of the Siege of Lathom House* (London: Harding, Mavor & Leopard, 1823); for Lyme Regis, see Colonel Were's daily account down to late May 1644 in the Earl of Warwick, *A Letter from the Right Honourable Robert, Earl of Warwick, Lord High Admiral of England* (London, 1644) and Edward Drake's daily account of the entire siege transcribed and printed in Arthur Bayley, *The Civil War in Dorset* (Taunton: Barnicott & Pearce, 1910); for Pontefract, see William Longstaffe, 'Nathan Drake's account of the siege of Pontefract Castle', *Miscellanea 1* (Durham: Surtees Society, 1861); for Scarborough Castle, see Jack Binns, *The Memoirs and Memorials of Sir Hugh Cholmley of Whitby, 1600–1657* (Woodbridge: Boydell, 2000); for Worcester, see Stephen Roberts, Stephen Porter and Ian Roy, *The Diary and Papers of Henry Townshend* (Bristol: Worcestershire Historical Society, 2015).

10 At The National Archives [hereafter TNA], SP28, in the so-called 'Commonwealth Exchequer Papers'.

the modest size of the garrison – probably well under 300 men in total – it is clear that they lived and dined very well.

This impression is confirmed by the records of the garrison's expenditure – rather than allowances for goods and services taken in lieu of taxes due. There were payments to bakers, smiths, tilers, messengers and guides, for horses and other military equipment, and for extra provisions, including eggs, beer, sack, radishes, turnips, kale, carrots, parsley, 'salads out of the country,' mustard, pepper, sugar, 'hard cheese for the table,' apples, oranges, lemons, 'rathe [early] green peas,' rosewater, vinegar, eels, codfish, other fish, two dozen pigeons, salt, paper and ink, '4 Venice glasses for beer and wine,' earthenware vessels and a 'great…jug for the use of the table' and dishes for 'the new tables.' Other notable payments include those to gunsmiths who mended presumably old or broken muskets which the garrison had collected from the surrounding area, to a tailor who made a new coat for the garrison's porter, to a woman who served as the garrison cook until she was dismissed, to 'spies' sent off to report on sieges or enemy garrisons, as well as 'to a woman that came from Sir Tomas Fairfax privy and was to go to Bristol for intelligence', to workmen who fitted out a little lockable closet with shelving for the clerk's use, cut a hatch in the storehouse door and made 'the bower in the meadow', to men who 'buried the garbage about the house', to the soldier who cleaned 'the hall and tables where the soldiers go to meals', for pitch and tar 'to mend the boat' used for fishing in the moat, as well as to men who cleared 'logs and rubbish' from the moat, for medicines acquired from Bath and other medical supplies, unguents and 'apothecary ware' and for the woman who washed the table linen. The governor clearly lived in some style, as he was supplied with plenty of ordinary and worm-wood beer, wine and sack, he acquired several tobacco pipes and he had his clothes washed for him at the garrison's expense.

Overall, the impression might be of a very comfortable, rather leisurely lifestyle for the governor, officers and men at Great Chalfield House, and one which meant that significant sums of money were being ploughed back into the local economy, partly balancing the cash, goods and services being taken from it to support the garrison. Instead of horrors and brutality, it is seductively easy to conjure up an image almost of domestic bliss in this corner of civil war Wiltshire. On the other hand, Great Chalfield House was at the time close to Royalist territory and on the fringes of a contested area, which may help to explain why ready cash was so limited and why, as the income accounts record, little or nothing could be received from areas 'lying remote from the garrison and lying under the enemy's principal garrison of the Devizes.' The accounts also show extra payments to soldiers 'for their work' and 'for laying of turf and other labour' at the time 'when the enemy lay about the house', for 'strong water that the governor had taken in when the enemy lay about the house' and also for 'a shroud for a wounded soldier that died.' The garrison evidently came under attack at least once and, perhaps on that occasion, at least one of the soldiers had been fatally wounded. Moreover, there was clearly plenty of sickness and disease in the garrison throughout the period covered by these accounts, given how frequently they record expenditure on the care and diet of the sick.[11] A plush and cosy gentlemen's club it was not.

At Great Chalfield and elsewhere, we can reconstruct something of daily life within a fortified stronghold from the extant financial accounts which it maintained. At a handful of sites, the surviving siege diaries and their like enable us to reconstruct something of how that life changed dramatically when a stronghold came under attack. That document dependant and driven approach has been the traditional way in which historians have studied garrisons, strongholds, fortifications and sieges in the civil war. But in recent years – and in the main the focus this volume – there has been a huge expansion in studying these and other aspects of the war through the physical remains which they have left. The use of landscape and landscape history to enhance our understanding of particular battles and campaigns is, of course, nothing new. It is clear that Samuel Gardiner and Charles Firth visited some of the battlefields of the Civil War and that their written interpretations drew on and benefitted from that – admittedly, probably quite limited – fieldwork. That approach was taken much further in the series of monographs of individual civil war battles initiated by, and in some cases written by, Peter Young and published by the Roundwood Press during the 1960s and 1970s,[12] and it underpins and informs many recent battlefield studies.[13] But over the last generation or so, the role of archaeology and architectural history and studies of Civil War battles, sieges and fortifications informed by finds made in the ground, and through close investigation of standing remains, has burgeoned.[14]

This new approach can create some tensions. Much of the 'archaeology' in fact involves the systematic, and all-too-often not so systematic, use of metal detectors

---

11 The original set of accounts survive at TNA, SP28/138/18. The full transcript by John Pafford, *Accounts of the Parliamentary Garrisons of Great Chalfield and Malmesbury, 1645–46* (Devizes: Wiltshire Archaeological and Natural History Society Records, 1940).
12 For example, Peter Young, *Edgehill, 1642: The Campaign and the Battle* (Kineton: Roundwood Press, 1967), Peter Young, *Marston Moor, 1644: The Campaign and the Battle* (Kineton: Roundwood Press, 1970), Peter Young and Margaret Toynbee, *Cropredy Bridge, 1644: The Campaign and the Battle* (Kineton: Roundwood Press, 1970) and John Adair, *Cheriton, 1644: The Campaign and the Battle* (Kineton: Roundwood Press, 1973).
13 Such as Christopher Scott, Alan Turton and Eric Von Arni, *Edgehill: The Battle Reinterpreted* (Barnsley: Pen & Sword, 2004), Glenn Foard, *Naseby: The Decisive Campaign* (2nd edn, Barnsley: Pen & Sword, 2005) and Malcolm Wanklyn, *Decisive Battles of the English Civil War* (Barnsley: Pen & Sword, 2014).
14 For excellent insights into or overviews of work of this type, see the three studies by Harrington cited in fn. 8, Glenn Foard and Richard Morris, *The Archaeology of English Battlefields* (Oxford: Council for British Archaeology, 2012) and Glenn Foard, *Battlefield Archaeology of the English Civil War* (Oxford: Archaeopress, 2012).

to find and locate the spread of Civil War related metallic artefacts on a site. Duly plotted out on a map of the battlefield, the results have sometimes been used to suggest radical new interpretations about where the armies initially deployed, how the engagement unfolded or where the fiercest fighting took place. These can be a little controversial and where they conflict with the standard interpretation built upon *solid and substantial information* found in extant contemporary documents, by no means all civil war historians have been convinced that we should privilege the new metal detectorist evidence.[15] Again, the reporting of some new archaeological finds tends to be overblown and to exaggerate their importance, sometimes quite wildly.[16] However, at its best, used with care and employed in conjunction with the contemporary written and printed sources, evidence gleaned from archaeology and the scrutiny of standing architecture can substantially enhance our understanding of particular civil war sites, actions and engagements, including the role of fortifications, as the ensuing chapters amply demonstrate.[17]

***

15 For example, the suggestion that at Edgehill the two armies deployed not on a south-west to north-east alignment, parallel with the Edgehill escarpment, as most historians relying on the surviving documentary sources have argued, but instead closer to a north-south alignment or even a north-west to south-east alignment, an interpretation resting largely on the spread of metallic finds by metal detectorists on parts of this (much altered) battlefield, have not convinced everyone. For this new interpretation, see Foard and Morris, *Archaeology of English Battlefields*, fig.7.22, but note that the caption accompanying the map does stress that it offers a 'conjectural reconstruction' of the armies' deployment and that 'significant uncertainties remain' given the very disturbed nature of the terrain in the wake of MOD use and building work.
16 A good example is much of the reporting in early 2023 of civil war era stonework found at an excavation at Coleshill Manor in Warwickshire, allegedly linked to the 'nearby Battle of Curdworth Bridge' and which 'may rewrite the history of the English Civil War.' The coverage in the *Guardian* was fairly typical: <https://www.theguardian.com/uk-news/2023/jan/21/coleshill-towers-remains-history-english-civil-war> [accessed 8 August 2023]
17 Some of the best recent published work of this type, blending documentary, archaeological and architectural evidence and findings, explores the civil war defences built or repaired around garrisoned towns. For example, the recent work on the civil war defences of Chester and Gloucester discussed below, together with an outstanding fresh study of the defences of another county town in the Marches, Jonathan Worton, '"The Strongest Works in England?" The defences of Shrewsbury during the civil wars, 1642–1651', *Transactions of the Shropshire Archaeological and Historical Society*, 87 (2014). For an early but fascinating use of archaeological evidence to reconstruct life in a garrisoned castle, see Lawrence Butler, *Sandal Castle, Wakefield* (Wakefield: Wakefield Historical Publications, 1991), pp.86–103, where ceramic finds from the period, including cooking vessels, kitchen ware and chamber pots, have been plotted out in order to indicate where within the castle each smaller unit of the garrison troops was based, cooked, ate and passed their time.

Just how fortified strongpoints might shape the course of the conflict and the unfolding campaigns and fighting during the civil war can be illustrated by comparing and contrasting the role and impact of the two garrisoned and refortified towns at either end of the Welsh Marches. Chester and Gloucester had, and indeed still have, much in common. Both began life as Roman legionary forts, founded in the 60s or 70s AD, their defensive circuits quickly upgraded to stone, with a classic 'playing card' ground plan and with a regular grid-iron layout of streets within the fort.[18] Both were founded close by the lowest easily bridgeable stretch of major rivers, tidal at that point, before they opened out into wider estuaries. From the outset, therefore, both developed port areas and served as centres for overland but also water-borne movement and trade, the latter entailing riverine and inter-coastal as well as longer distance shipment of goods. Both were largely abandoned after the withdrawal of the Roman army and administrative system and became semi-ruinous, before being refounded as defended towns or burghs by the Saxon Kingdom of Mercia in the closing centuries of the first millennium AD. Both went on to become flourishing towns and ports in the medieval period, defended by an enlarged circuit of medieval stone walls and gates, in part following the line and footprint and incorporating some of the fabric of the much earlier Roman defences, in part following a new route and so enclosing a larger urban area, in the process taking part of the new defensive circuit closer to the river and the port areas. Both also gained medieval castles, initially Royal castles established by William I, shortly after the Conquest. In both, much of the Roman grid-iron regular street pattern was retained and persisted throughout the medieval period and beyond. By the eve of the civil war, both Gloucester and Chester had become established county towns, administrative and judicial centres, and also religious centres with a cathedral and at the heart of a wider diocese; both retained significant stretches of their medieval defences, in the form of stone walls and gates, and both were flourishing market centres and active west coast ports. The populations of both towns in the Tudor and early Stuart period were broadly comparable, at around or a little over 5,000,[19] most of whom lived within the medieval core, though by that time both towns had gained extra-mural suburbs.

At first glance, the position and role of both of these key Marcher towns during the main Civil War of 1642–46 seems remarkably similar, albeit with the sides reversed. After a period of initial uncertainty and hesitancy right at the start of the Civil War, Gloucester was then quickly secured for Parliament; after a period

18 However, Gloucester was soon degarrisoned and became a Roman civilian centre and town, while Chester, though spawning civilian settlement and services outside its walls, remained a legionary fort and military base throughout the Roman period.
19 At times probably peaking at over 6,000, though then falling back through the repeated visitations of plague and other epidemics from which both towns suffered.

of initial uncertainty and hesitancy right at the start of the war, Chester was quickly secured for the King. Thereafter, garrisons – whose numbers fluctuated in the course of the war, but generally numbered in the high hundreds or over a thousand in each – were installed in both towns, the existing defences around the urban core were repaired and upgraded and attempts were also made to defend at least some of the extra-mural suburbs. As it turned out, both towns continued to be held by the side which secured them in the early days of the war until the end, or very near the end, of the conflict. Thus Gloucester remained in Parliament's hands throughout, while Chester was retained by the King until its surrender in February 1646, just a few months before the first civil war ended. However, at several points during the war, both towns came under great pressure and it seemed very possible that they would fall. Both found themselves on the front line, close to a frontier between Royalist controlled and Parliamentarian controlled territory. Thus Chester was under pressure from spring 1643, when Parliamentarian forces secured most of the rest of Cheshire; thereafter, Royalist control of Chester and the hold of its long-time governor – John, Lord Byron – was far from secure and Chester endured attack, blockade or close siege for much of the rest of the war. Meanwhile, Gloucester was under great pressure from summer 1643, when the Royalists expanded their control over the West Country and the South-West Midlands, overrunning almost the whole of Gloucestershire, and so marooning and surrounding the County town; thereafter, Parliamentarian control of Gloucester and the hold of its governor, Sir Edward Massey, seemed very precarious and Gloucester endured attack, blockade or close siege for much of the rest of the war. In short, the wartime histories and fortunes of these two, in many ways very similar, Marcher towns seem almost identical, albeit with the positions reversed – Royalist Chester threatened by Parliamentarian control of the region, Parliamentarian Gloucester threatened by Royalist control of the region.[20]

---

20   For general studies of Gloucester in the civil war, see Malcolm Atkin and Wayne Laughlin, *Gloucester and the Civil War: A City Under Siege* (Stroud: Alan Sutton, 1992) and, in its county and wider context, Andrew Warmington, *Civil War, Interregnum and Restoration in Gloucestershire, 1640–72* (Woodbridge: Boydell, 1997) and John Wroughton, *An Unhappy Civil War: The Experiences of Ordinary People in Gloucestershire, Somerset and Wiltshire, 1642–46* (Bath: Lansdown Press, 1999). For general studies of Chester in the civil war, see John Barratt, *The Great Siege of Chester* (Stroud: History Press, 2003), 'Early modern Chester 1550–1762: the Civil War and Interregnum, 1642–60', in Christopher Lewis and Alan Thacker (eds), *A History of the County of Chester: Volume 5 Part 1, the City of Chester: General History and Topography* (London: Victoria County History, 2003), Peter Gaunt, 'Chester's Role in the Civil War', *Cromwelliana* (1995) and, in its county context, Peter Gaunt, 'The Civil War in Cheshire: a Unique Experience?', *Cromwelliana* (2019). Operations in both towns and counties are explored from a Royalist perspective within Ronald Hutton, *The Royalist War Effort, 1642–46* (2nd edn, London: Routledge, 1999).

However, when we dig a little deeper, significant differences begin to open up in the wartime records of the fortified towns and their garrisons. In particular, the contemporary sources point to an apparent and very stark contrast between the seemingly dynamic and aggressive Parliamentarian garrison at Gloucester under Edward Massey and the apparent inaction and defensive mode of the Royalist garrison in Chester under its successive governors.[21] That sentence, laced with words of caution such as 'apparent' and 'seemingly', has been carefully constructed, for we need to be cautious and to ensure that the appearance of Gloucester's dynamism contrasting with Chester's caution is not a false impression created by the undoubted disparity in the quality and quantity of the surviving contemporary source material. In general, the extant wartime Parliamentarian sources are very much fuller, richer and more plentiful than surviving Royalist or pro-Royalist sources and that is certainly true when we focus on Cheshire and Gloucestershire and their two county towns.

The Parliamentarian commander in Cheshire who led the operations against Chester, Sir William Brereton, and Edward Massey as wartime governor of Gloucester were both very good at self-publicity, at directly or through others feeding the editors and journalists who compiled the regular London-based, pro-Parliament newspapers of the war years and at having their actions lauded in, and their slant on military developments conveyed through, the plentiful pamphlets of the day. For example, Brereton's campaign across Cheshire of late winter and spring 1643 was praised in a London pamphlet gushingly entitled *Cheshires Successe, Since their Pious and Truly Valiant Collonell Sr. William Brereton Barronet, Came to their Rescue Set Forth in 4. Chapters*,[22] while in the following year a pamphlet breathlessly recounting a clutch of successful military operations in Gloucestershire recently mounted or led by Massey appeared with the exuberant title *Eben-ezer. A Full and Exact Relation of the Severall Remarkable and Victorious Proceedings of the Ever-Renowned Colonell Massy, Governour of Gloucester.*[23] Many of the texts of Brereton's and Massey's wartime letters survive,

---

21 Sir Nicholas Byron in the early stages of the war, through to his capture in March 1644, and then, after the appointment of Francis Gamul proved abortive, for the remainder of the civil war and thus through the important period when Chester came under intensified Parliamentarian pressure, Sir Nicholas Byron's nephew, John, 1st Baron Byron.
22 *Cheshires Successe, Since their Pious and Truly Valiant Collonell Sr. William Brereton Barronet, Came to their Rescue Set Forth in 4. Chapters* (London, 1643); the title page carries the date 27 March.
23 *Eben-ezer. A Full and Exact Relation of the Severall Remarkable and Victorious Proceedings of the Ever-Renowned Colonell Massy, Governour of Gloucester* (London, 1644); the title page carries the date 4 June.

as copied into the letter-books of the Committee of Both Kingdoms.[24] Additionally, several of Brereton's own letter-books are extant and are readily accessible through modern published calendars,[25] while Massey's wartime activities were recorded and extolled in a lengthy account written by his chaplain John Corbet, which was printed and published towards the end of the war.[26]

Sir Edward Massey, as shown in a collection of images of Parliamentarian generals originally issued in 1647 and reprinted several times since. Despite his heroic defence of Gloucester, Massey later because disenchanted with, and alienated from, the Parliamentarian cause and by the early 1650s had become an active Royalist, fighting for the King at the Battle of Worcester, where he was badly wounded and captured, although he survived and later escaped. (Public domain)

24 Now at TNA, SP 21/16 and 17, covering the months June to September 1644 and September 1644 to February 1645 respectively. These two letter-books and thus letters written by as well as to and about Brereton and Massey are calendared within William Hamilton (ed.), *Calendar of State Papers Domestic, Charles I: Volume 19, 1644* (London: HMSO, 1888) and Volume 20, 1644–45 (London: HMSO, 1890).

25 Norman Dore (ed.), *The Letter books of Sir William Brereton* (2 volumes, Stroud: Record Society of Lancashire and Cheshire, 1984 and 1990), covering January to May 1645 and June 1645 to February 1646 respectively and thus focusing on his operations in Cheshire and against Chester. A further letter-book, from 1646 and calendared by Ivor Carr and Ian Atherton (eds), *The Civil War in Staffordshire in the Spring of 1646: Sir William Brereton's Letter Book, April–May 1646* (Stafford: Staffordshire Record Society, 2007), explores Brereton's final military operations outside Cheshire, against three strongholds in neighbouring Staffordshire.

26 John Corbet, *An Historicall Relation of the Military Government of Gloucester: from the Beginning of the Civill Warre betweene King and Parliament to the Removall of Colonell Massie from that Government to the Command of the Westerne Forces* (London, 1645). It

From the same set of contemporary engravings as above, Sir William Brereton, Parliament's commander-in-chief and County 'boss' of Cheshire, or at least the majority of the County that was in Parliamentarian hands from spring 1643 onwards. Although his sometimes glittering military and political careers quickly fizzled out once the Civil War was over, unlike Massey he remained loyal to the Parliamentarian cause in subsequent years. (Public domain)

In stark contrast to this Parliamentarian feast, there is Royalist famine, as is quite usual for the civil war. Perhaps Royalist wartime bureaucracy and record keeping at a local level was simply not as thorough as that maintained by their opponents, perhaps when the Royalists lost the war such records as they had maintained were deliberately destroyed or scattered and discarded as the King's cause went under, or perhaps it was a combination of both. But the result is that very few Royalist financial accounts generated by their armies, garrisons and local administrators, of the type which are quite plentiful on the Parliamentarian side, are now extant.[27] While the King did set up printing presses in Oxford and put

was, in effect, reissued two years later in a very slightly revised format under the partly new title of *A True and Impartiall History of the Military Government of the Citie of Gloucester: from the Beginning of the Civil War between the King and Parliament, to the Removall of that Most Faithfull and Deserving Commander for the Defence of his Country in their Greatest Necessity, Col. Edward Massey: who was Removed from that Government, to the Command of the Western Forces, where he Performed Most Faithfull and Gallant Service* (London, 1647).

27 For a rare survival of Royalist financial accounts, those compiled by the Royalist garrison in Lichfield, see Ian Atherton, 'Royalist Finances in the English Civil War: the case of Lichfield garrison, 1643–45', *Midland History*, 33 (2008).

out some wartime publications and propaganda, most notably a semi-regular newspaper, the output was quite limited and massively overshadowed by the array of pro-Parliamentarian newspapers, pamphlet literature and printed material churned out by the London presses.

It is certainly true that the leading Royalists operating in and around Gloucestershire and attempting to capture the County Town and the senior Royalist officers and governors defending Chester have left few financial accounts, correspondence, writings and contemporary printed matter of the sort which the Parliamentarians left in relative abundance. However, there is a dearth but not a complete absence of material reporting from the Royalist side or at least from a Royalist viewpoint in Gloucestershire and Chester. Sufficient survives from the Royalist officers operating in and around Gloucester to confirm that, shorn of some of its self-glorifying language and exaggeration, the stories told by Massey and by his chaplain were essentially true. Similarly, sufficient Royalist material survives from Chester, notably Lord Byron's own account of his governorship and defence of Chester,[28] corroborated by other lesser Royalist sources from within Chester such as the writings of Randle Holme or Holmes,[29] to confirm that the picture painted of Byron and his garrison by Brereton and the other Parliamentarian sources is in essence true. Thus the disparity in the activity of the two garrisons is no mirage; the aggression of the Gloucester garrison contrasting with the inaction and defensive mode generally adopted by the Chester garrison is no chimera but is supported by solid contemporary evidence.

Having been shut up and completely surrounded within Gloucester by a huge, though ultimately unsuccessful, Royalist siege overseen by the King in person, for several weeks during the summer of 1643, even after that direct pressure abated Massey and his garrison remained marooned and isolated in a sea of Royalist territory for the best part of two more years. Even once the tight siege was over and the King moved on, the town remained far from secure. As Corbet put it, 'this Garrison [was] was left to bear the brunt, provide for itselfe, and run the danger … not of another siege, yet of blocking up and ruine by the spoyle of our Countrey, which that party decreed to destruction; and the Enemy at the doore and the distance of our friends did threaten no lesse.'[30] Nevertheless, Massey 'was not satisfied in keeping his own Garrison, but eager of continuall service, to destroy

---

28 Bodleian Library, Rawlinson ms. B.210; with minor errors and omissions, it was transcribed and printed in instalments in *The Cheshire Sheaf*, 4th series, no.6 (1971).
29 His extensive archive, much of it reflecting on Chester, survives in the British Library, Harley mss; for his record of life and experiences in wartime Chester, see particularly Harley ms. 2125.
30 Corbet, *Historicall Relation of the Military Government*, p.54.

or disable the enemy.'[31] His objective, according to his chaplain, was 'to master the Country then enthralled to the enemy, yea, to lie upon the enemies quarters, consume their store, distresse their cheife Garrisons … and endanger the rest … and stop their supply of men and money.'[32]

This was big talk for a fairly small, and certainly dangerously isolated, garrison, but by and large that is what happened. From autumn 1643 until he moved on to a wider field command in spring 1645, Massey and his Gloucester garrison were remarkably bold and ingenious in taking the fight to the Royalists who dominated the County and the region. Despite the size, number and potency of the garrisoned strongholds in the King's hands nearby, extending their power 'on all sides almost to the Gates of Gloucester', Massey and his 'small party by continuall action upheld their repute',[33] repeatedly raiding and forcing out larger Royalist garrisons and attacking Royalist convoys. As Corbet further noted, '[t]he Garrison neverthelesse did not only defend its own territories, but made sundry adventures and inrodes upon the Enemies quarters, staved off, and kept them within their bounds.'[34] Massey made life very uncomfortable for the local Royalist forces, whether in the open or tucked up in fortified strongholds, launching surprise dawn attacks, raiding and striking and catching their enemies unaware, requisitioning and arming a frigate which they then used to launch water-borne attacks on startled Royalist garrisons who 'never dreamed of an enemy from Gloucester, in that corner of the Land, at such a distance.'[35] They pushed westwards, across the Severn, and into the Forest of Dean, capturing Monmouth, Usk and Ross; northwards, capturing Tewkesbury and Evesham and raiding Ledbury; eastwards, capturing Sudeley, Malmesbury and Cirencester; and southwards, capturing Berkeley, Beverstone and Tetbury. Massey suffered occasional reverses, though nothing major and crushing, and many of the places he captured he could not then hold and had to withdraw. But overall it was a glorious record, full of aggression and initiative, and as Corbet, perfectly fairly if slightly ungrammatically, put it, '[t]he Governour choosed rather to make work for the enemy, and to seek him in his own quarters, then [i.e. than] lie at home to expect the challenge.'[36] In the process, during the 20 months or so between autumn 1643 and early 1645, Massey and his men fought over 20 significant skirmishes or battles and were involved in a similar number of sieges and storms.

31 *Ibid.*, p.55.
32 *Ibid.*
33 *Ibid.*, pp.56, 60.
34 *Ibid.*, pp.66–67.
35 *Ibid.*, p.67.
36 *Ibid.*, p.69.

Meanwhile, the Royalist governor and his garrison at Chester were nowhere near as active or aggressive. Byron was very good at defending Chester as it came under growing Parliamentarian pressure in 1644–45, fiercely beating off Brereton's attacks on the northern outworks and, even once the Parliamentarians had taken the eastern suburbs and had opened up a breach in the stone wall in September 1645, repulsing the attempted storming which followed. In the end, only shortage of supplies and the pressure brought to bear by the civilians within the walled town, now shattered as a result of artillery and mortar bombardment, induced Byron to open negotiations, leading to the peaceful surrender of Chester in February 1646. However, during its long lifespan, the Chester garrison only rarely moved much beyond the town's defensive circuit and its immediate hinterlands taking the war to its opponents, and then only briefly, and generally not very successfully, when others took the lead or forced them on – in mid-winter 1643–44 when Byron was ordered to lead reinforcements newly arrived from Ireland out on a wider county campaign, which within four weeks came to grief at the Battle of Nantwich, or in September 1645 when the King instructed part of the garrison to sally out to support a Royalist relief army on and around Rowton Moor, with equally disastrous consequences. Beyond defending and retaining Chester itself, which Byron and his men accomplished with considerable success, the record of achievement of the Chester garrison in the wider region was very thin, bordering on desultory or embarrassing.

All this begs the obvious question of why, despite their seemingly very similar positions, the Parliamentarian garrison in Gloucester was so active and outgoing, in a way that the Royalist garrison in Chester conspicuously was not. A number of explanations can be advanced, some of which shed light on the nature and consequences of civil war defences and fortifications. Others, however, are not so physical.

Morale within the garrison and amongst its defenders is one obvious intangible but crucial factor. The numerous minor but generally successful and rewarding operations mounted by the Gloucester Parliamentarians from autumn 1643 onwards helped to keep up their morale, despite their isolation. As the governor's chaplain noted, '[t]hese little services were answerable to the times, and upheld the esteem of the Garrison in that low ebbe'; having 'fetched its livelihood out of the fire' and succeeded in 'keep[ing] the enemy in action, and prevent[ing] their extravagances', the garrison was able 'to beare up the hearts of our friends, and signifie to the world that we were yet alive.'[37]

Conversely, one of the few occasions on which Chester's Royalist garrison took to the field, bolstered by reinforcements from Ireland to mount a mid-winter

---

37 Ibid., pp.67, 68–9.

campaign across the County in December 1643 and January 1644, culminated in disaster when the Siege of Nantwich ended with catastrophic defeat at the hands of Sir Thomas Fairfax. The Royalists lost around 300 dead and 1,500 captured and many more deserted or changed sides. The strength of the garrison at Chester had been numerically depleted, but more important the stuffing seems to have been knocked out of the surviving troops and their officers and morale flagged. The letters written by Lord Byron and his brother in the wake of the Battle of Nantwich have a defeatist air about them, abounding with phrases such as '[i]t hath pleased God to turn the tide of our good fortune here' and 'our whole actions have been nothing but disasters.'[38] In the light of that attitude, it is little wonder that the garrison looked inwards and focussed on their own, and Chester's, defence.

We might also consider the leadership qualities of the various governors. Despite some negative character traits, some of which emerged somewhat later in his career, Massey is described by a recent biographer as possessing 'a mixture of outstanding qualities of military leadership, courage, sheer luck, and a talent for publicizing himself' and this account of his leadership of Gloucester is littered with adjectives such as 'dashing' and 'defiant'.[39] In contrast, Sir Nicholas Byron's biographer sees his time in charge of Chester as 'a limited success, marred by feuding between Byron as military governor, the townsmen, and the local Royalist gentry' and notes that as early as spring 1643 he was urging a defensive Royalist strategy, not engaging their enemies in England but instead falling back into the West and awaiting substantial reinforcements from Ireland.[40] Even Lord Byron's more positive pen portrait stresses his shortcomings, too, noting 'his intelligence, impatience, enterprise, arrogance, brutality, and administrative efficiency' and suggesting that even 'when every allowance is made for misfortune, disadvantage, or misrepresentation, he still seems deficient in the career for which he is chiefly remembered, as a soldier.' Thus '[w]hile he could clearly hold a position with the utmost determination and resource', his role as a commander in the field and in wider battles and campaigns is judged much more harshly and his limitations and failings are stressed. 'As such,' the author concludes, 'his part in the defeats and missed opportunities of the Royalist cause, at both national and regional level, is likely to remain rather more memorable than his role in its successes.'[41] That is a

---

38   Thomas Carte (ed.), *A Collection of Original Letters and Papers Concerning the Affairs of England from the Year 1641 to 1660* (2 volumes, Dublin: William Ross, 1759) I, pp.36, 39, 40.
39   Andrew Warmington, 'Massey [Massie], Sir Edward (1604x9–1674)', *Oxford Dictionary of National Biography* [hereafter *ODNB*], online edition at <https://www.oxforddnb.com/> [accessed 8 August 2023].
40   George Herby, 'Byron, Sir Nicholas (*bap.* 1596, *d.* 1648)', *ODNB*.
41   Ronald Hutton, 'Byron, John, First Baron Byron (1598/9–1652)', *ODNB*.

judgement that could be applied perfectly to his rather supine and defensive stance while in command at Chester.

Massey could be a very prickly character and during his time as governor of Gloucester he clearly fell out with several other regional commanders and Parliamentarian administrators. Nonetheless, he and the town benefitted both from the military efforts of Sir William Waller, Parliament's principal general in the region during the first half of the war, and from the political and wider support provided by Parliamentarian county committees elsewhere in the region, such as Warwickshire, and from the Parliament sitting in London. In contrast, Sir Nicholas Byron had to work with the rather lacklustre regional commanders appointed by the King during the first half of the war, notably Sir Thomas Aston and Arthur, Lord Capel,[42] while Lord Byron found himself for a time having to play second fiddle to Prince Rupert as regional commander, which had its own disadvantages, as the Prince repeatedly drained troops and resources from the Chester garrison in order to supply his own field army. Moreover, the King's rival Oxford Parliament was a rather desultory and limited body and, even during its fairly short lifespan, in practice it did little to support Chester and other key Royalist provincial towns and garrisons.

Turning to rather more physical and geographical factors, we also need to think about the environs of the two towns and their garrisons. Gloucester might gain support and succour from Parliamentarianism within the region. On the English side, although members of the landed elite in eastern Gloucestershire and the Cotswolds seem to have been predominantly Royalist-leaning, there was clearly plenty of popular Parliamentarianism there, as evidenced by the treatment of the Royalist Lord Chandos and his coach when he sought to rouse support for the King in Cirencester early in the war.[43] To the west, in the Forest of Dean area, the acquisitive and overbearing policies pursued in the pre-war years by the courtier and Catholic landowner Sir John Winter (or Wintour), from 1638 private secretary to Queen Henrietta Maria, probably produced a pro-Parliamentarian reaction among the ordinary foresters, iron workers and coal miners of the Forest.[44] Massey and his garrison might also have benefitted from heightened and broader anti-Catholicism in a region which saw itself as vulnerable to Irish Catholic attack via the Severn Estuary, especially in the wake of the King's truce

---

42   See E.C. Vernon, 'Aston, Sir Thomas, first baronet (1600–1646)' and Ronald Hutton, 'Capel, Arthur, First Baron Carpel of Hadham (1604–1649)', *ODNB*.
43   Nicholas Poyntz, 'The Attack on Lord Chandos: popular politics in Cirencester in 1642', *Midland History*, 35 (2010).
44   Andrew Warmington, 'Winter, Sir John (b. *c.*1600 d. in or after 1676)', *ODNB*.

or Cessation concluded with the Irish Catholic rebels in summer 1643.[45] Although popular feeling over the border in Wales had initially been distinctly Royalist, as the war went on general exhaustion and disillusionment set in and the allegiance of the Welsh began to waver. In the latter half of the war, Massey – like several Parliamentarian commanders along the Marches, most notably Sir Thomas Myddelton further north – began to woo the Welsh, apparently with some success, treating Welsh prisoners with kid gloves:

> the Governor entreated [them] kindly, and after a few dayes sent them home by parcels, and each man with a little note or letter directed to his master, or the severall Parishe, to signifie that the intention of the Parliament, and the present government, was not to destroy, or enslave their persons, or take away their livelihoods; but to preserve their lives and fortunes, to open the course of justice, & free them of their heavy burthens under the forces of Rupert a Germane Prince.[46]

In contrast, the Royalist opponents of Massey and his Gloucester garrison were often weak or divided. The presence of the great Royalist bases of Bristol and Oxford not too far away served as a distraction and, once the big push to capture Gloucester by close siege in summer 1643 had failed, those two cities were far more attractive for ambitious Royalist officers than slogging away in a rather dour campaign in Gloucestershire. The strongly and overtly Catholic complexion of the Royalist military leadership in west Gloucestershire and over the border in Monmouthshire, as epitomised by Winter, Marquess of Worcester and his son Lord Herbert (who became Second Marquess in 1646 on his father's death in 1646), disquieted many fellow Royalists. That several other senior officers who operated in Gloucestershire, men such as Nicholas Mynne and Sir William Vavasour, had either Catholic or Irish links did nothing to unify the Royalist war effort in the region.[47]

---

45 Corbet certainly claimed that news of the Cessation and the subsequent presence of troops from Ireland within Royalist forces active in the surrounding area produced a local reaction in favour of Parliament, which boosted Massey's recruitment drives, *Historicall Relation of the Military Government*, pp.63–64.
46 *Ibid.*, p.112.
47 Stephen Roberts, 'Somerset, Edward, Second Marquess of Worcester (d.1667)', *ODNB*; Andrew Warmington, 'Vavasour, Sir William, baronet (d.1659)', *ODNB*, who not only quotes Corbet's judgement that he was 'complained of, reviled and cursed and at once lost every opportunity of action and advancement in the King's service' but also himself notes that Vavasour 'fell foul of Herbert, who resented being sidelined, while Sir John Winter, Governor of the Forest of Dean, and Colonel Nicholas Mynne, his former lieutenant-colonel, increasingly ignored his orders'.

The position of Royalist Chester and its garrison was very different. On the one hand, to the east they faced a fairly united Parliamentarian enemy. There was little sign there from spring 1643 onwards of any groundswell of popular royalism which might afford succour to the garrison; on the contrary, there is plenty of evidence of a hardening line against royalism in much of Cheshire in the wake of the King's Cessation and of the brief but brutal rampage through much of the County, undertaken by reinforcements newly brought over from Ireland in mid-winter 1643–44. The Parliamentarian military and administrative war effort in Cheshire was under the firm and unified command of Parliament's County boss, Sir William Brereton, who in effect had an independent command and so rarely found himself forcibly distracted and his resources depleted by orders to campaign elsewhere.[48]

However, the Royalists within Chester had one advantage which Massey certainly did not possess. From 1643 to 1645 Gloucester was effectively surrounded by Royalist controlled territory and was isolated, with no reliable or secure landline for supplies and reinforcements to get in. That compelled the garrison for its sheer survival to take to the field in order to raid Royalist convoys and bases in the surrounding area. As Corbet put it, '[t]hus was the City pestered on every hand, and fetched its livelihood out of the fire, with continuall hazard, forcing the enemies quarters.'[49] Chester was very different, for while it was hemmed in by hostile territory and under attack on its eastern (Cheshire) side, until very late in war it enjoyed good, easy and unchallenged communications with a solid block of Royalist territory to the west, in North-Eastern and more generally North Wales. As the war dragged on, the Royalist outlook of that region came under increasing strain and there was a growing chorus of complaint and criticism, with pleas of poverty and exhaustion and that the resources of Denbighshire and Flintshire should no longer be drained away to supply Royalist bases such as Chester across the border in England.[50] However, those supply lines remained open, until the closing stages of the war Chester could be kept supplied and equipped from North Wales and hence, unlike Massey and his men in Gloucester, Byron and his garrison could sit back and were not compelled to take to the field and to campaign further afield in order to keep themselves fed.

That difference in the position of the two garrisons was underlined and cemented by the immediate physical context, the natural and man-made defences of Gloucester and Chester during the Civil War. On at least two grounds, Chester's

---

48 John Morrill, 'Brereton, Sir William, first baronet (1604–1661)', *ODNB*.
49 Corbet, *Historicall Relation of the Military Government*, p.68.
50 See Peter Gaunt, 'The Nursery of the King's infantry? Reassessing the civil war in Wales, 1642–46', *Cromwelliana* (2023), especially pp.39–41.

natural defences were far more potent and effective than those of Gloucester. First, Chester was defended on two sides by a wide, deep, partly tidal and non-fordable stretch of the River Dee, whose single crossing point by the town, the (Old) Dee Bridge, was easily defendable. In contrast, the Severn really only protected one corner of the historic core of Gloucester, while also running by one side of the western suburbs. Second, Chester itself is built on a dome of sandstone, by no means lofty or very pronounced, but sufficient to ensure that it is not overlooked by any significantly higher ground nearby. Most of central Chester is around or a little over 100 feet, or 30-odd metres, above sea level and one would need to travel several miles in any direction before encountering the 150 foot contour, with the substantially higher ground of the Sandstone Ridge 10 miles away at its nearest point. By contrast, most of central Gloucester is around 60 feet or 20 metres above sea level, but it is overlooked by much higher ground nearby, including Robins Wood Hill at 650 feet, or around 200 metres, less than 2 miles (3.2 kilometres) from the centre of the town and Churchdown Hill at just over 500 feet, or 154 metres, within 3 miles (4.8 kilometres) of the centre; additionally, the North-Western edge, or escarpment, of the Cotswolds, rising to over 600 feet (200 metres) overlooks the town less than 5 miles (8 kilometres) away. In addition to its much more limited riverine defences, therefore, in terms both of its general position and of being within range of the most potent artillery pieces of the time mounted on higher ground, Gloucester was significantly weaker and more vulnerable than Chester. The strength of Chester's position almost encouraged the governor and his garrison to sit back, confident that they were secure and could take what their enemies could throw at them, in a way that the governor and garrison of Gloucester could not. Perhaps that encouraged the latter to be far more outgoing and active, determined to take the fight to their enemies well beyond the environs of Gloucester.

Those defensive differences become even more pronounced when we turn to the man-made defences. As indicated by the Speed map of Chester, drawn up a generation before the Civil War, and confirmed by written sources of the pre-war and war years, seventeenth century Chester had retained a complete circuit of standing medieval stone walls. They needed refurbishing and repairing when peace gave way to war in the early 1640s, with some gateways closed up, the main gates updated, the outer ditch redug and so forth. Additionally, the extra-mural suburbs north and east of the historical core were given some protection through new outer lines of earthen bank and ditch constructed during the first half of the war, before then being either deliberately abandoned and flattened by the defenders (the northern line and suburb) or falling to Parliamentarian assault (the eastern line and suburb, in September 1645) in the later stages of the war. However, the crucial point is that the historic core and the majority of Chester

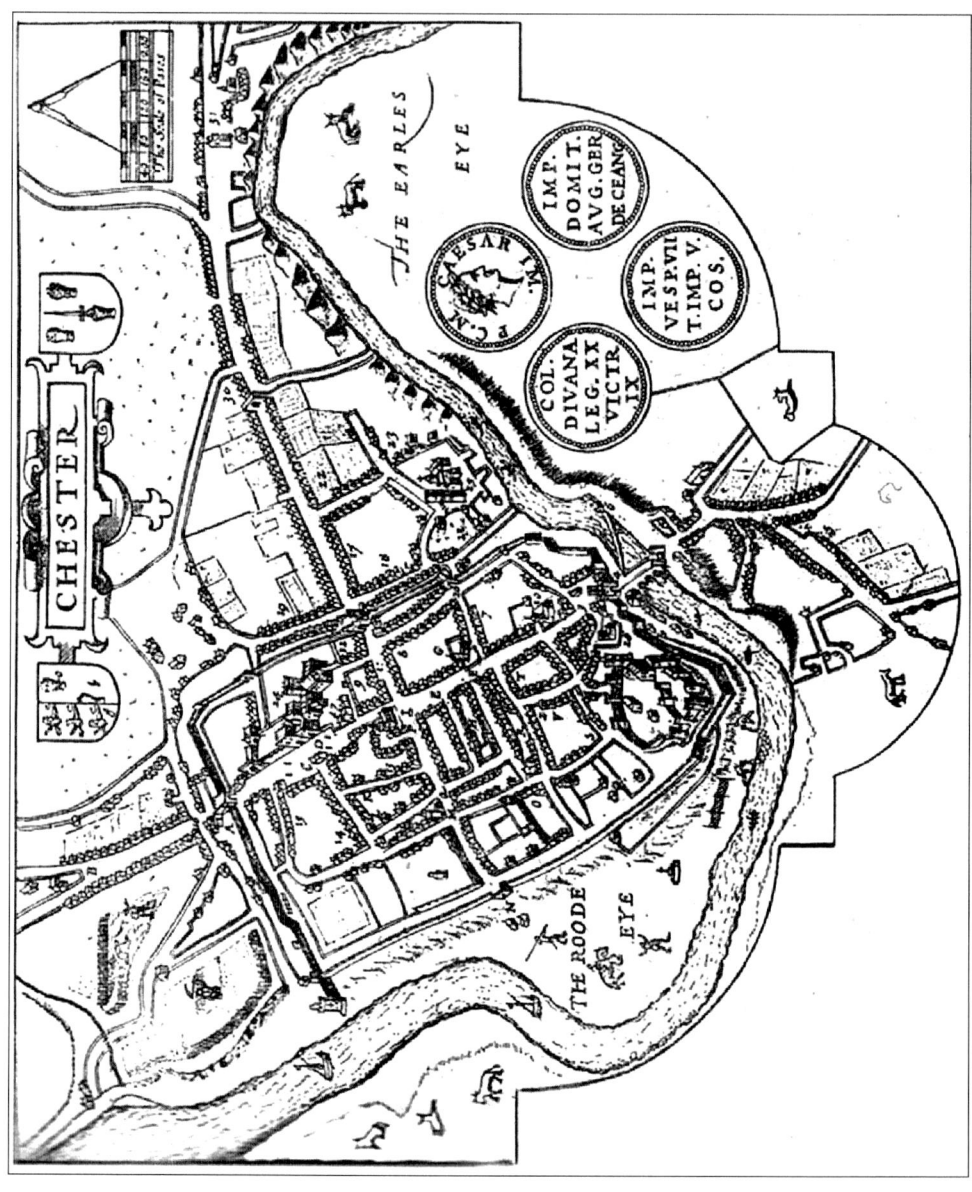

Speed's map of Chester, which adorned his county map, depicts the town in the pre-war years. It brings out how, in the early Stuart period, Chester was enclosed and defended on two sides by the looping River Dee and, apart from the extra-mural suburban growth, on all sides by a still-complete and quite uniform circuit of stone walls and gates. (Public domain)

were robustly defended by a complete circuit of potent masonry walls and gates from the beginning of, and throughout, the civil war.[51]

The core of medieval Gloucester was protected by a complete, or nearly complete, circuit of stone walls, pierced by gates, though the circuit was probably never as clear and uniform as that at Chester; thus parts of the northern line were made up of the outer walls of other properties and institutions, including Gloucester Abbey and St Oswald's Priory. Moreover, although there are documentary references to repairs being undertaken in the opening decades of the seventeenth century, Speed's town map appears to show some stretches of the wall either ruinous or less strongly defended than other stretches. Corbet certainly pulled no punches in describing the lamentable state of Gloucester's defences on the eve of the Royalist siege of 1643, even though by that point some repairs and upgrading had been hastily undertaken, including the creation of some earthworks and earthen batteries:

> The works of a large compass, not halfe perfect; ... thence to the Northgate, with a slender work upon a low ground ... from the North to the West-gate, (being a large tract of ground) there was no ancient defence, but a small work newly raysed, with the advantage of marish grounds without ... From the West towards the South gate along the River side, no more defence then [than] the River it selfe, and the meadowes beyond levell with the Town.[52]

The town's defences were progressively upgraded in the course of the remainder of the war, initially to repair the significant damage wrought by the Royalist bombardment during the siege of summer 1643, which included wrecking two gates, then or later moving on to the construction of new earthwork bastions to strengthen and protect the main gates, the installation of new drawbridges and the upgrading and strengthening of several stretches of the existing stone walls.[53]

---

51   The best general historical survey of the walls and gates of Chester is 'Major buildings: city walls and gates', in Alan Thacker and Christopher Lewis (eds), *A History of the County of Chester: Volume 5 Part 2, the City of Chester: Culture, Buildings, Institutions* (London: Victoria County History, 2005). Despite some minor discoveries made since it appeared, the best study of Chester's man-made defences during the civil war remains Simon Ward, *Excavations at Chester: The Civil War Siegeworks, 1642–46* (Chester: Chester City Council, 1987).
52   Corbet, *Historicall Relation of the Military Government*, p.41.
53   The best and most recent account of Gloucester's wartime defences, reproducing and interpreting a contemporary plan of the defences discovered in 2012, and incorporating new archaeological finds as well as using the contemporary documentary sources, is John Rhodes, 'The Civil War Defences of Gloucester', *Transactions of the Bristol and*

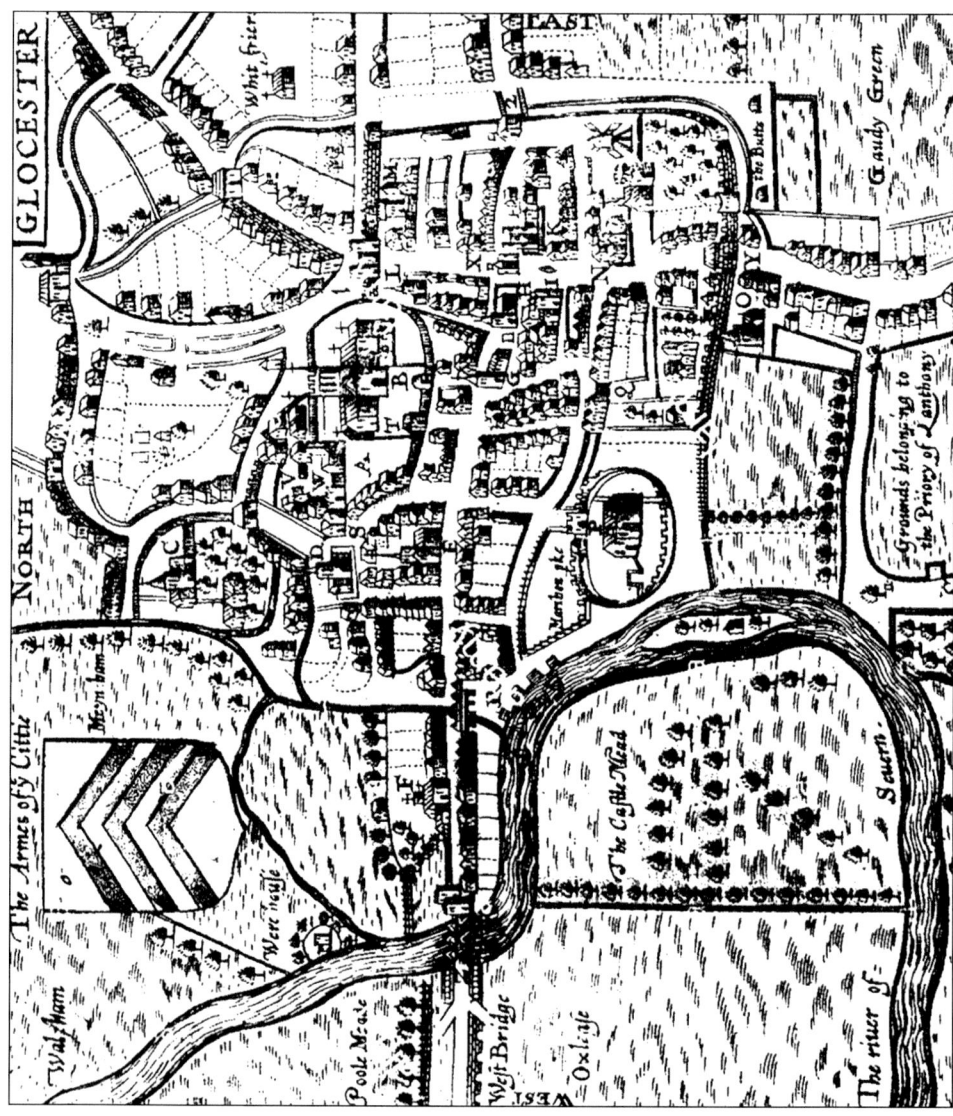

Speed's map of Gloucester, again adorning his county sheet, shows very significant stretches of medieval walls and defences still standing when the map was drawn in the early seventeenth century, but they lack the clear and uniform circuit evident on his map of Chester. In places, the walling seems to be irregular, quite insubstantial, incomplete or even absent. (Public domain)

Nonetheless, it is fairly clear that the man-made defences of Gloucester during the Civil War were always lagging behind, and were less robust and complete, than those of wartime Chester. Once more, therefore, these factors may have encouraged Byron to sit back and absorb his enemies' onslaughts, but persuaded Massey that his main hope lay in a more forward and aggressive form of defence, keeping his opponents well away from Gloucester.

The womb big with many miseries, conjured up by the anonymous pamphleteer of early 1643, had visited Gloucester and Chester in full measure as the war had progressed, as it had so many other towns and villages, manor houses and churches fortified during the civil war and caught up in the conflict. As it did so, and as the chapters which follow amply demonstrate, the miserable spectacles and the sad relations of war had become all-too evident. The so-called water poet and versifying travel writer, John Taylor, undertook a 600-mile tour around parts of England and Wales in summer 1652, his route bringing him through both Chester and Gloucester, his birthplace, though the resulting travelogue he published the following year said disappointingly little about either. But he was far more revealing about the sad condition of another county town in the Marches he had passed through, whose medieval walls, gates and castle had been refurbished during the war as a Royalist stronghold and to house a Royalist garrison, besieged and eventually compelled to surrender in the dying days of the main civil war.

> On Fryday the 30. of *July* [1652], I rode (and footed it) ten Miles to *Flint* (which is the Shire Town of Flint-shire) and surely War hath made it miserable, the sometimes famous Castle there … is now almost buried in it's own Ruins, and the Town is so spoiled, that it may truely be said of it, that they never had any Market (in the memory of man) they have no Sadler, Taylor, Weaver, Brewer, Baker, Botcher, or Buttonmaker; they have not so much as a signe of an Ale-house, so that I was doubtfull of a Lodging … and this (me thinks) is a pitifull discription of a Shire Town.[54]

Gloucestershire Archaeological Society, 132 (2014). This partly though not entirely supersedes earlier work, including the broader account 'Gloucester: Bridges, Gates and Walls', in Nicholas Herbert (ed.), *A History of the County of Gloucester: Volume 4, the City of Gloucester* (London: Victoria County History, 1988), Atkin and Laughlin, *Gloucester and the Civil War*, Malcolm Atkin, 'David Papillon and the Civil War Defences of Gloucester', *Transactions of the Bristol and Gloucestershire Archaeological Society*, 111 (1993), exploring Papillon's grand and never fully executed plans of 1646 to hugely upgrade the town's defensive circuit, and Malcolm Atkin and Russell Howes, 'The use of archaeology and documentary sources in identifying the civil war defences of Gloucester', *Post-Medieval Archaeology*, 27 (1993).

54   John Taylor, *A Short Relation of a Long Journey, Made Round or Ovall by Encompassing the Principalitie of Wales, from London, Through and by the Counties of Middlesex*

Such were the terrible consequences of bitter territorial warfare, the civil war of fortified and garrisoned strongholds and of siege, bombardment and storm, which England and Wales had endured in the 1640s.

and Buckingham, Berks, Oxonia, Warwick, Stafford, Chester, Flint, Denbigh, Anglesey, Carnarvan, Merioneth, Cardigan, Pembrooke, Caermarden, Glamorgan, Monmouth, Glocester, &c. (London, 1653), p.10.

The Siege of Moreton Corbet Castle

A case study of the archaeological evidence of attack and defence at a small garrison siege of the War of the Three Kingdoms

Richard Leese

The Siege of Moreton Corbet Castle in September 1644 was a relatively minor affair in the overall story of the Wars of the Three Kingdoms. A Royalist garrison of around 80 men were overcome in a surprise night assault, in perhaps less than an hour of fighting from the first shots being fired, by a Parliamentary force of less than twice their number. A satellite of the Royalist garrison at Shrewsbury, its fall was an indicator of the turn of the war in Parliament's favour in Shropshire in late 1644, and a portent for the eventual fall of Shrewsbury in February 1645. Today Moreton Corbet Castle stands as a ruin under the custodianship of English Heritage, having been abandoned as a residence by the Corbet family for over three centuries. This paper is a summary of doctoral research carried out by the author in conjunction with English Heritage between 2013 and 2019 as part of establishing a methodology for the examination of the evidence of attack and defence at siege sites of the civil wars in England, for which Moreton Corbet was the case study site.[1]

Siege actions have been relatively overlooked by developments in battlefield and conflict archaeology since the first systematic metal detector survey of a battlefield at the Little Bighorn in the 1980s. An assessment of the state of 'siegefield archaeology' by Peter Harrington in the mid–2000s intimated that part of the problem lay in the visibility of structures and earthworks at siege sites, and

---

1   Richard J. Leese, *Siege Archaeology of the English Civil Wars: Establishing a methodology to unlock the archaeology of attack and defence at early modern siege sites* (University of Huddersfield, 2020), Doctoral Thesis.

Eastward view of the ruined Elizabethan range at Moreton Corbet Castle, Salop. (Author's photo)

that these have typically drawn attention away from the potential of the types of unstratified evidence, typically artefacts deposited by the exchange of small-arms and artillery fire and other objects dropped during the fighting, that were being increasingly explored for battlefields.[2] Harrington's assessment was that small siege sites were deserving of greater archaeological attention due to their potential for surviving unstratified archaeology and bullet impact evidence. Yet despite this no systematic study of these elements of historic siege archaeology for the seventeenth century had been undertaken prior to the commencement of the study of Moreton Corbet Castle.

2   Peter Harrington, 'Siegefields: An archaeological assessment of 'small' sieges of the British civil wars', *Journal of Conflict Archaeology*, 1 (2005), pp.93–113.

What is a siegefield?

A siegefield is the archaeological landscape encompassing the area within which a historic siege action was fought. While no formal definition exists for what constitutes a siege action, the definition utilised by the author considers a siege to be: '… a distinct military action against an occupied defensive position where control of the position through displacement, removal or elimination of the garrisoned force, or the destruction of the position are the main objectives of the attacking force, and where the garrison resist this attack.'[3]

This definition was specifically constructed to incorporate actions that would traditionally be considered stormings rather than sieges. While an assault by storm seldom required the preparation of trenches or lines of circumvallation by the attackers, the weaponry and military culture underpinning their conduct is the same for these actions as for static sieges, with the same intended objective and the same kind of target regardless of the duration or scale of such actions.

The evidence within a siegefield may include a variety of components depending on the duration of the siege, the tactics utilised by the attackers, and the circumstances of the defended site. These might consist of extant fortifications and earthworks, stratified remains of destroyed buildings and trenches, occupational evidence from the garrison, and extant or ruined structures present at the time of the siege. Archaeological methodologies already exist for exploring the majority of these components, such as the use of excavation for stratified features including buried fortification earthworks, siegeworks and gallery mines, for example.

Though methodologies for the exploration of the unstratified evidence of battlefields existed prior to this study, these had yet to be applied systematically to completion for a siege site. The detector survey at Grafton Regis in the 1990s was the closest example; however it was never fully completed because of the demanding level of intensity of the survey for the volunteer detectorists.[4] Bullet impacts on extant or ruined structures have been recognised as physical traces of past conflict since at least the late nineteenth century,[5] but these too lacked previous study in detail or a methodology for their investigation. It is these two forms of evidence that the doctoral research carried out by the author sought to redress through the Moreton Corbet study.

---

3   Leese, 'Siege Archaeology', pp.20–21.
4   Glenn Foard and Richard Morris, *The Archaeology of English Battlefields: Conflict in the Pre-Industrial Landscape* (York: Council for British Archaeology, 2012), p.137.
5   Foard and Morris, *The Archaeology of English Battlefields*, p.128.

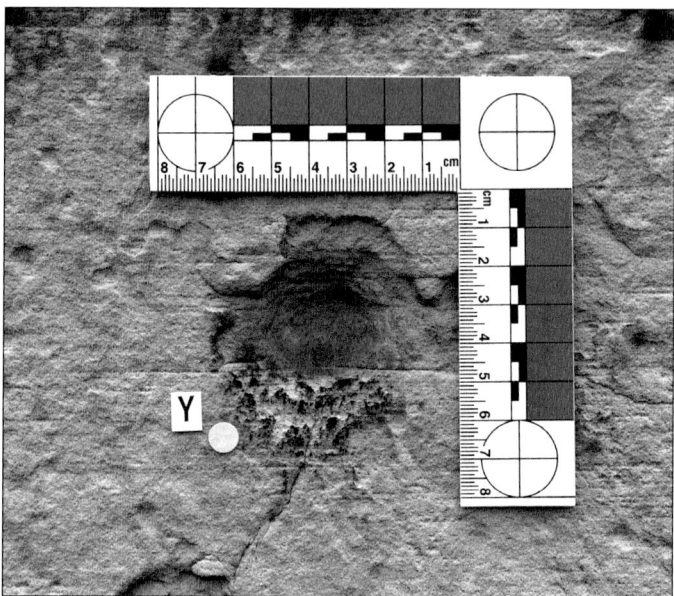

A typical small-arms impact scar at Ashby de la Zouch Castle, Leicestershire. (Author's photo)

What are impact scars?

An impact scar is a three-dimensional cavity in the surface of a dressed stone block arising from the impact of a bullet, either from an artillery piece or from a handheld, small-arms weapon. The terminology here is important; these are not 'bullet holes' in that they do not perforate the surface of the stone. Instead these are the resulting features created by the fragmentation or displacement of surface material on the stone wall behind the point of contact, which has then been subjected to almost 400 years of exposure to weathering processes.

There are relatively few identified archaeological examples of artillery impacts that have produced a coherent scar on the surface of a stone structure, with the majority of identified artillery-shot impacts usually taking the form of fragmented or dislodged masonry. This is likely in part due to the higher impact energies of large calibre artillery bullets, but also the projectile material, namely iron, which is less malleable compared with lead bullets and thus retains its shape for longer during the impact process, causing greater damage to the contact-point. By contrast small-arms impact scars have been identified in significant quantities at a little less than half of all siege and garrison locations examined by the author during on-site investigations.[6] They are usually only visible on dressed stone surfaces, i.e. ashlar with a flat or regularly-shaped outer facing. Impact scars have yet to be positively identified on rough stone surfaces. Some small-arms impact damage has been tentatively identified on brick structures adjacent to Basing House, Hampshire, but these also do not leave a uniform or coherent scar.

Despite the wide range of different stone types upon which impact scars were formed across geographically disparate sites, they nevertheless share a selection of common features between them. These are broken down into three components; the inner scar, outer spalling and radial fracturing.

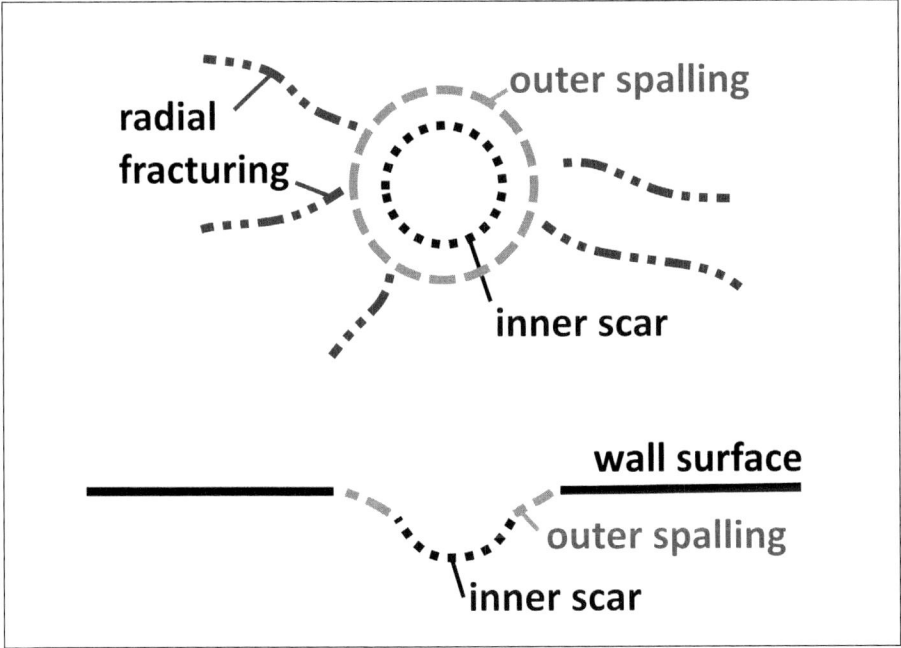

Diagram of the typical features of a small-arms impact scar.

The inner scar is a recess into the stone surface that corresponds to the original surface point of impact of the projectile. It is formed through a combination of stone material directly displaced by the impact process, and the gradual loss of the weakened and exposed sedimentary stone behind the point of the impact. It is

6   Leese, 'Siege Archaeology', pp.47–48.

typically approximately hemispherical in shape, and often shows a much lighter internal surface colour to the outer face of the surrounding stone.

The area of outer spalling is an area of fragmentation of the stone surface immediately surrounding the inner scar which has been displaced either through the deformation of the bullet at the time of impact, or through fragmentation of the stone surface that has then been dislodged. The spalled area surrounding a scar is not always present for small-arms impact scars, either because it has not formed, or because weathering has weakened its distinctiveness from the inner scar shape. For observed small calibre, lead-projectile artillery impacts an area of spalling is always present, and for larger iron-projectile impacts the spalling is often present surrounding the damaged or dislodged masonry, despite the lack of a coherent inner scar.

Radial fractures appear as shallow fissures in the impacted surface, radiating away from the inner scar and outer spalling, and often following bedding planes in the stone. These fractures pass throughout the internal stone structure and often lead to catastrophic surface material loss where impacts occur close to the edge of a stone block. Where these fractures intersect the surface, weathering exaggerates and deepens their overall appearance into shallow grooves. Radial fractures are less common for most small-arms impact scars, but are nearly always visible around the edge of larger scars and are present for all identified artillery impacts, suggesting that they may be an indicator of higher relative impact energy.

Impact scars are not unique to siege locations, with stone structures in locations of known skirmishes and in some cases battles showing evidence of small-arms impacts.[7] Nevertheless, the prevalence of stone-faced structures in the location of sites garrisoned during the Wars of the Three Kingdoms means that for many siege actions, these buildings were at the centre of offensive fire from small-arms and artillery, and occasionally also on the receiving end of defensive fire over the course of a developing engagement. Despite being at the centre of firefights however, small-arms impact scars are seldom clustered around openings such as doorways and windows on these structures. Instead they typically occur in a range of heights, most commonly between 1m and 3m above ground level, indicating that the majority of impacting bullets were being fired at targets located outside of those structures.[8]

For skirmishes this is a natural product of the fluid form of engagement, as opposing soldiers are seldom in fixed positions, or may be using intervening obstacles as cover. For sieges however, it initially seems counterintuitive that defending soldiers should not be using the buildings as cover, until considering

---

7   Foard and Morris, *The Archaeology of English Battlefields*, pp.128–134.
8   Leese, 'Siege Archaeology', p.110.

A small calibre artillery impact at Old Wardour Castle, Wiltshire. (Author's photo)

that most prepared defensive positions in this period consisted of earthwork fortifications.[9] The reason for this scar distribution in the case of sieges is that the buildings are merely the backdrop for shots fired at soldiers passing in front of the structures, or in defended positions beyond the walls of the building. Only at sites where the building has been actively used as a fighting position do scars appear clustered around natural target points, and where this occurs, such as at Old Wardour Castle in Wiltshire, the evidence is particularly striking.

9   Christopher Duffy, *Siege Warfare: The Fortress in the Early Modern World 1494–1660* (London: Routledge, 1979).

Impact scars from shots targeted at a window opening at Old Wardour Castle, Wiltshire. (Author's photo)

While three-dimensional digital laser-scanning would be the ideal method of recording and preserving impact scar data, this was not feasible with the equipment available to this study. Instead a low-cost manual method of recording the cross-sectional profile of scars was devised utilising a pin contour-gauge and acrylic recording-frame, tracing pin-pressed cross-sectional profiles onto graph paper for later measurement off-site.[10] Macro photography was used to record the overall location of scars on a structure and for translating these into an elevation diagram for positional measurement in GIS software, while individual scars together with reference numbering were photographed for the visual appearance of the scar.

Profiles were recorded for scars across a sample number of sites to test for statistical correlations in scar shape and form. While generally scars showed a correlation for increase in feature size with the overall size of the scar, individual scars displayed variations in elements such as the overall scar shape, size and deepest-point offset from centre. This suggested that there may be impact variables, such as velocity, bullet size and overall direction of impact, that translate into formation of the shape of the scar. If the relationship between the impact variables

10   Leese, 'Siege Archaeology', pp.96–99.

and the overall scar shape could be identified, this would allow greater analysis of individual archaeological scars.

No prior experimental research has explored the formation processes of impact scars created by small-arms projectiles from the early modern period. Although forensic science provides groundwork for investigating ballistic impacts for modern-era firearms, this does not directly translate onto impacts on dressed stone that have weathered over four centuries. Some unpublished ballistic studies have touched upon musket ball impacts on stone surfaces; although these produced datasets of limited value for investigating the impact scars themselves. What these experiments seemed to indicate however is that the shape of a scar is almost entirely formed at the moment of impact, and the subsequent crater is then weathered to the softened appearance of an archaeological scar over time.

An experiment devised by the author was carried out in partnership with the Yorkshire Shooting Centre in Mirfield, West Yorkshire in March and April 2019. This experiment was designed to create a series of impacts under controlled conditions that would allow comparison of variation in the cross-sectional profile between freshly created impact scars with varying angles of bullet impact. The experiment used stone blocks of equal size, transported from the local quarry in Huddersfield, and set at a fixed range from the delivery weapon. Bullets of a single calibre were loaded into shotgun cartridges that had been pre-loaded with a fixed quantity of gunpowder to produce consistent muzzle velocities for impacts.[11]

After initial test impacts however, it was discovered that the stone did not produce scars with any cross-sectional depth, but instead produced surface marks consisting of lead smearing with an infusion of lead and pulverised sandstone grains in the centre that was vulnerable to contact. Although the sandstone sourced was harder than that used in prior studies, one significant consideration was that this stone had been subjected to several months weathering in the quarry outdoor storage yard prior to acquisition. It had thus undergone some degree of case-hardening of the outer surface prior to the experiment, a factor that was deliberately sought for authentic stone-response to impact for this experiment but had apparently been overlooked in previous impact experiments.

The aims and objectives of the ballistic trial were thus rapidly redesigned to measure and record the initial marks after formation, examine the recovered bullet fragments and assess their relationship to each impact mark, and allow the impact marks to weather naturally over time to observe and assess how they relate to the scar formed after a period of weathering.[12] Two sets of marks were formed at different impact velocity ranges across a set of 15 stone blocks,

---

11   Leese, 'Siege Archaeology', pp.147–151.
12   Leese, 'Siege Archaeology', pp.151–166.

producing 30 experimentally-formed impact marks. Two pairs of scars were taken from the total of 30 and subjected to immediate pressure-washing to examine the full depth and profile of the impacts with the loose material artificially removed.[13] The remaining 26 impacts were left in an outdoor location exposed to natural weathering processes. After four years of weather exposure the exposed impacts are visually catching up to the pressure-washed examples and are already beginning to resemble examples from siege sites, though with a rougher internal surface texture than the archaeological scars. These blocks will continue to be exposed to weathering with their progress monitored over time to examine their further development; however the extremely long-term influence of weathering on the development of these impact scars on a par with seventeenth century example will be beyond the capacity of this author to investigate fully. Further impact experiments utilising different stone types and re-examining the issue of variables such as angle of impact will be needed before the potential of individual impact scars will be fully understood for archaeological investigation.

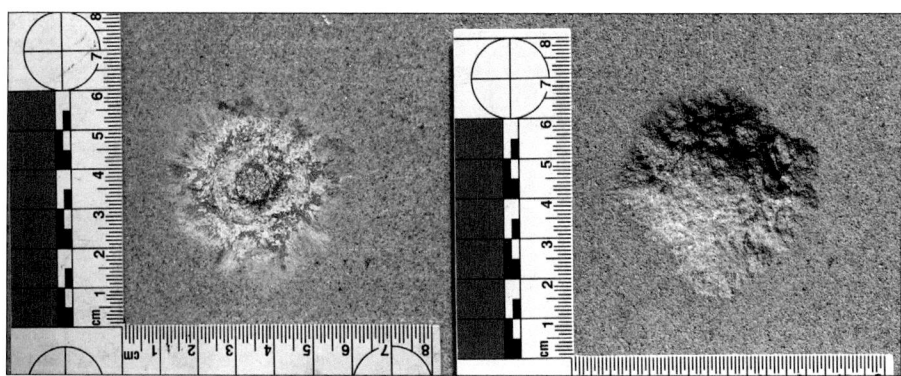

Left: A fresh musket ball impact on a sandstone block. Right: The same impact after four years of weather exposure. (Author's photo)

Moreton Corbet Case Study

Prior to two redevelopments in the sixteenth century, Moreton Corbet Castle began life as a late twelfth century moated stone castle. The first of the sixteenth century developments was an effort by Sir Andrew Corbet in the 1560s to transform the castle into a 'modern' two-storey residence, of which only the gatehouse and

---

13   Leese, 'Siege Archaeology', pp.160–165.

garderobes survive in the ruins today. After Andrew's death in 1579, his son Robert Corbet began the construction of the Italian-style Elizabethan southern range.[14] Undeniably the most imposing element of the structure even today in its ruined condition, this grand range was apparently unfinished upon his untimely death in 1583, and Robert's successor chose to live elsewhere. By 1623 it was inherited by Sir Andrew's grandson and namesake, and was both furnished and inhabited, with construction work by that stage having finished, even if the extent of Robert's designs had not been fully realised.[15]

When war broke out in England in 1642 the then owner of the estate and Member of Parliament, Sir Vincent Corbet (great-grandson of Sir Andrew), declared for King Charles and raised his own regiment of dragoons for the royalist cause.[16] It is unclear when the castle became fortified, almost certainly no later than 1643, at which point Wem had been taken and fortified for Parliament. The castle most likely served as the barracks for Corbet's dragoon regiment, with the Corbet family taking residence instead at Acton Reynald estate, just a mile and a half away to the west.[17]

A history of the castle by Paul Remfry suggests that it was captured by Parliament in January-February 1644, as correspondence from Sir Vincent in late February 1644 requests permission for a prisoner exchange for soldiers taken from the castle during a storming.[18] Other than this reference however, no contemporary account of an engagement or the surrender of the castle garrison from this period of the war has been identified. The castle was certainly back in royalist hands again by some time around March 1644 – until the events of September that year. Royalist fortunes in the region were beginning to turn sour in late 1644, and the fall of Montgomery Castle on 5 September 1644 proved a significant regional blow. A royalist force was dispatched from Shrewsbury to retake Montgomery, including Vincent Corbet's dragoons,[19] and ultimately met defeat at the Battle of Montgomery on 17 September 1644. It was during this absence of the dragoons from Moreton Corbet Castle that it was taken by Parliament.

In the early hours of the morning of 8 September 1644 a Parliamentarian detachment of around 140 musketeers and dragoons from William Brereton's

14 Elain Harwood, 'Moreton Corbet Castle', *English Heritage Historical Review*, 1 (2006), pp.37–40.
15 Harwood, 'Moreton Corbet Castle', p.43.
16 Paul M. Remfry, *Moreton Corbet Castle, 1066 to 1700* (Worcester: SCS Publishing, 1999), p.25
17 Jonathan Worton, *To Settle the Crown: Waging Civil War in Shropshire 1642–1648* (Solihull: Helion & Company Ltd, 2016), p.109.
18 Remfry, *Moreton Corbet* Castle, p.26.
19 Remfry, *Moreton Corbet* Castle, p.26.

forces stationed in the north of the county, and under the command of Colonel William Reinking, took Moreton Corbet Castle by storm. A small group of soldiers led personally by Reinking breached the earthen fortifications using ladders before the alarm was raised, taking the garrison force by surprise and forcing them to fall back to the castle. The assault party managed to fight their way through the fortifications and force entry into the castle, causing the garrison of about 80 soldiers to surrender in fear of the consequences of being overrun. The entire engagement probably took no longer than an hour, and eliminated a satellite garrison positioned almost half-way between the major Parliamentary garrison at Wem and the Royalist garrison in Shrewsbury.

Two accounts of the capture of Moreton Corbet Castle in September 1644 survive from the period, neither of them being first-hand, and both from the perspective of the Parliamentarians. The first and shorter account, published in the Parliamentarian newsbook *The Weekly Account* in 1644, relates basic details of the capture, including the size of the attacking force and its commander, the means and method of the assault, some detail about the nature of the defences, and details of the number of captured soldiers and quantity of supplies taken from the garrison.[20] The second and more elaborate account published by Vicars in another Parliamentarian chronicle, *The Burning-bush Not Consumed*, in 1646 contains much of the same information, but adds details such as the use of codewords and subterfuge to distract the sentry, the use of the castle windows as firing positions by the defenders, and the use of grenades by the attackers. The two sources also disagree on the point of entry into the castle by Reinking, with *The Weekly Account* referring to entrance through a small door, while Vicars relays that Reinking and his detachment forced entry by breaking a mullion in one of the windows.[21]

The castle remained largely intact following the siege and was garrisoned by Parliament, likely until the fall of Shrewsbury in February 1645, after which point the royalist threat in northern Shropshire had been largely eliminated. The castle was repaired and possibly even reoccupied as a residence after the civil wars, but by the late seventeenth century the family had permanently moved their seat to Acton Reynald, where the Corbet family continue to reside to this day.[22] The castle gradually fell into ruin over the following three centuries and the grounds and ruins themselves were used as agricultural land until the castle entered national custodianship in 1945, and today remains an unstaffed and free-to-access English Heritage site.

---

20   Daniel Border, *The Weekly Account* (Issue 56) (London: Bernard Alsop, 1644), pp.446–447.
21   John Vicars, *Magnalia Dei Anglicana* (London: J. Rothwell and T. Underhill, 1646), pp.24–25.
22   Harwood, 'Moreton Corbet Castle', p.44.

The archaeological investigation of the Moreton Corbet siegefield sought to answer a number of questions about the siege that arise from the accounts and the visible evidence in the landscape. Can the location of the historic defences be located and their nature be determined? Does the unstratified archaeology indicate areas of focus in the outgoing defensive fire from the garrison, and does this correspond with impact scarring on the castle and church? Can the location of the breach of the defences by the assault party be identified from artefact distribution? Can the impact evidence be used to indicate the probable location of attackers in the landscape? Does the archaeology support or contradict elements of the accounts of the siege?

Reconstructing the historic landscape at Moreton Corbet

Reconstructing the contemporary terrain at the time of the siege is a challenge in that there are no surviving maps from the period. The closest contemporary map that gives clues to the surrounding landscape is a 1748 estate map of the late Corbet Kynaston. It is clear from the estate map that even by the early eighteenth century the castle itself had become part of the farming landscape, as one of the field boundaries follows the exact outline of the walls of the structure. Few buildings are illustrated on the map which makes identifying the location of outbuildings related to the castle difficult, however the names given to various field divisions indicate the land surrounding the castle was largely used for livestock grazing. The terrain surrounding the castle was also most likely wet or waterlogged, as evidenced by the field names 'Deepmoor Meadow', 'Moor' and 'Pool Meadow'. During metal detector surveying it became clear that, despite the presence of nineteenth century drainage in the modern landscape, some lower-lying areas of the arable fields still become intensely boggy after sustained periods of rainfall. Other elements indicated by the map, such as 'Swines Wood' and the castle pond, are totally absent from the modern landscape.

Although the accounts of the siege refer to earthwork defences at Moreton Corbet, no trace of them above ground survives today. A clue to their possible location comes from a 1989 survey by Wilson-North to record the remnants of the castle garden earthworks before their loss to modern ploughing as the landscape began to be moved over to arable use.[23] In the survey Wilson-North noted features in the landscape that he identified as being corner features of the raised platform of

---

23   W. R. Wilson-North, 'Formal Garden Earthworks at Moreton Corbet Castle, Shropshire', in M. Bowden, D. A. Mackay and P. Topping (eds.), *From Cornwall to Caithness: some aspects of British field archaeology. Papers presented to Norman V Quinnell* (BAR British Series 209, Oxford: BAR Publishing, 1989), pp.225–228.

the castle gardens to the south of the Elizabethan range, describing them perhaps ironically as 'bastions'.[24] Although the contours in the transcribed map do not equate directly to the typical form of Civil War fortifications, it is reasonable to hypothesise that this raised platform surrounded by marshy ground could have formed the basis for defensive fortifications to the south of the castle.

Using the Kynaston estate map together with lidar data and the locations of contemporary listed buildings, an approximate map of the contemporary terrain at the time of the siege was constructed for Moreton Corbet. This map includes the speculative location and elements of the fortification circuit to the east and south based on data available from the gardens survey, but does not speculate on defences to the west of the castle and garden platform, where the contours become less clear or where the presence of modern farm buildings has removed any potential survival of earthworks.

Surveying the siegefield

Metal detector surveying of the fields surrounding Moreton Corbet began in September 2014 and concluded in April 2019. The survey was carried out by a team of archaeologists and volunteers using detectors set to non-ferrous detection mode, using a transect survey method. Transect spacings were initially placed at 10m intervals as was used for the majority of the Edgehill Battlefield survey in the late 2000s,[25] with the intention of re-detecting at 5m intervals in areas closer to the castle or showing higher density of artefacts.

It became apparent very quickly that this search density was producing very few significant objects for reasonable analysis, with the vast majority of objects recovered being fragments of demolition lead with embedded charcoal and signs of smelting. Calculations from the rate of recovery of lead bullets from the initial 10m survey indicated that if you extrapolate over the entire survey area, between 80 and 130 would be recovered from site, a sample size much too small to make reasonable analytical assessments.[26] It was decided that subsequently transect spacing would be reduced to 2.5m intervals to increase sample size and provide a better data framework for establishing a siegefield detecting methodology for future sites. For a battlefield site this degree of search intensity would not normally be feasible; however with the relatively compact survey area at Moreton Corbet (a total of 20.86 hectares) this was achievable, if somewhat laborious.

---

24 Wilson-North, 'Formal Garden Earthworks', p.226.
25 Glenn Foard, *Battlefield Archaeology of the English* War (Oxford: BAR Publishing, 2012).
26 Leese, 'Siege Archaeology', p.181.

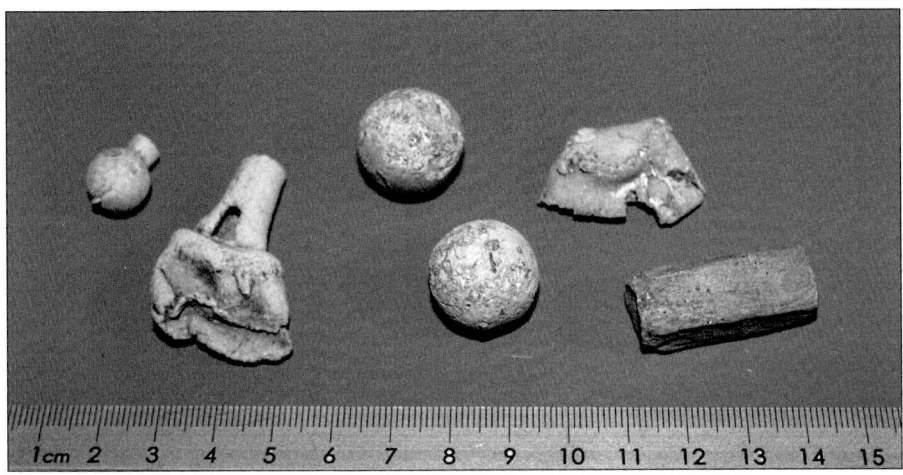

A sample of siege related artefacts recovered from the metal detector survey. (Author's photo)

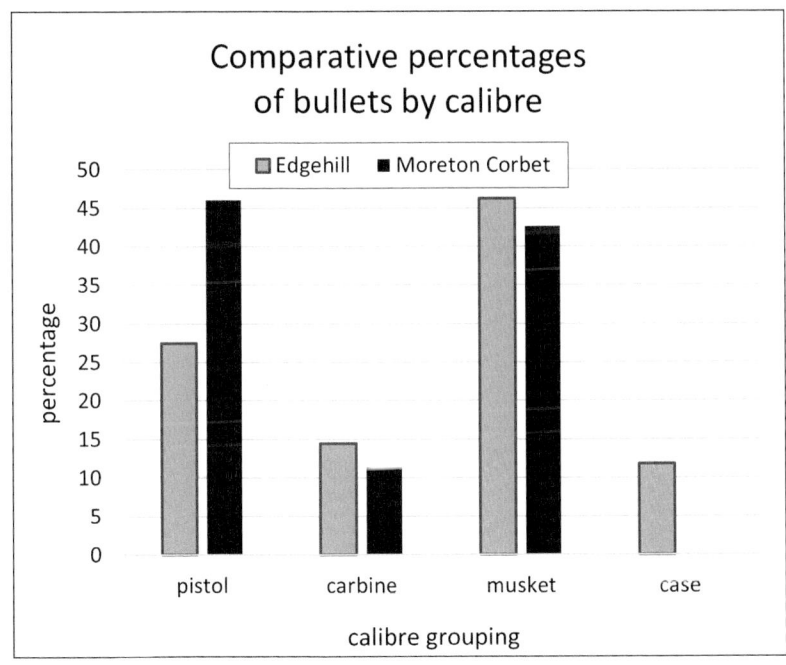

Percentages of recovered bullets by firearm calibre at Edgehill and Moreton Corbet. (Author)

The site was surveyed over 22 non-consecutive days across five years, resulting in a total recovery of 1,320 artefacts of all types, of which 268 were bullets or bullet fragments. A further 7 objects were of certain military origin of the period, including five bandolier powder-box caps and one priming-flask nozzle. In addition, two sprue fragments from gang moulds for bullets were found in the area of the gardens and just to the south garden platform, both for bullets of at most pistol calibre.

The above calibre percentages graph of bullets from Moreton Corbet compared with the totals for bullets recovered from Edgehill shows the variation in percentages of the total bullets for each calibre classification, though the total number of bullets for Edgehill is almost four times greater than the total recovered from Moreton Corbet. The most notable difference in the collections is the much higher percentage of smaller calibre bullets at Moreton Corbet. This may reflect a much higher degree of close-quarter firefights from the defenders against the assaulting force, or may simply reflect the weaponry used by the defenders, being presumably drawn from Corbet's dragoon regiment. The degree of background noise from later recreational shooting is unclear however; the site today is still actively used for recreational shooting, and early periods of this may account for a significant quantity of the bullets below approximately 28 bore.[27]

Within the distribution, three loose associations of bullets for musket and carbine calibres can be identified extending away from the castle, one to the south across the gardens and particularly densely clustered around the position of the hypothesised south-east corner of the fortifications. A second bullet-group extends away to the south-east, and another to the east, with a possible fourth in the field to the east of the church. Each of the five powder-box caps, items typically lost in use during fighting, are located within each of the first three associations of bullets, and four of these were recovered outside of the probable line of the defences, suggesting that these may have been dropped by soldiers in the attacking force, rather than by the garrison. The wide spread of the clusters of bullets fired outward of the defences would seem to indicate attack from multiple directions, which would corroborate the account given by Vicars that the attackers fired from multiple locations to indicate the garrison was under assault by a much larger force.[28] The association of bullets extending to the north and to the east side of the church may also indicate the use of the church as cover by a force approaching the castle, a hypothesis which is corroborated by the quantity of bullet impact scars on the castle-facing wall of the church.

---

27 Foard, *Battlefield Archaeology*, p.156.
28 Vicars, *Magnalia Dei Anglicana*, pp.24–25.

The impact scar survey of Moreton Corbet identified a total of 150 small-arms scars across both the castle and church structures, with a further 29 possible scars that could not be identified with certainty. The survey utilised the pin-gauge profile measurement methodology to record scars by number where accessible to reach using a step-ladder, and for those above attainable height, photography alone was used to record their position and allocate numbers in digital plotting.

While the cross-sectional profile cannot yet provide direct information about the impact or shot that formed these scars, their spatial context was analysed for clues relating to the origin of the impacts as a whole. As with most sites, there are no impacts at Moreton Corbet that show indication of being targeted directly at a doorway or window. This latter point would seem to discredit the account given by Vicars of the defenders firing from the castle windows, unless the specific windows in question are no longer extant on the ruined castle structure, or the attackers elected not to fire back at them. The prevalence of scars on areas of wall away from the surviving windows elsewhere on the castle would nevertheless seem to support the suggestion that the defenders did not use the windows as firing ports, and instead utilised the earthwork defences for their intended purpose.

With the exception of eight of the 49 scars identified on the church, all occur on walls facing the castle and garrison, suggesting that these were in fact caused by the defenders shooting at soldiers attacking from the direction of the church, and may be related to the bullet distribution in the field beyond the church to the north. Most of these scars occur at heights above ground level of 2m or more. When the change in ground level and obstacles between the castle and the church are considered, it is likely that this excessive height distribution is due to the stone wall of the churchyard providing covering from shots against the attackers. The impacts represent those shots that passed over the height of the wall having missed their targets and struck the church beyond. Unfortunately, the churchyard was extended closer to the castle sometime in the late nineteenth century, and the boundary wall was demolished and relocated at its current location. An examination of the new wall, on the possibility that material from the old wall could have been reused, could not identify any impact scars.

The majority of scar clusters on the castle are found on the eastern wall, in areas reciprocated by the bullet distributions extending away from the castle. On the southern wall however, a small cluster of 10 scars on a recessed section of wall, occurring either side of a now missing column base, provided an opportunity to assess probable angle of origin, based on the physical limits of the flight of the shots that led to those scars. Measurements were taken of three scars in close proximity to the projected location of the column base, with the cones of possible shot origin traced outwards in GIS mapping software to give an overlap. Strikingly, when plotted this overlapping area of possible shot origins passed through the southern cluster of recovered bullets, two of the dropped powder-box caps, and incorporated the south-east flanker of the speculative defences.

An attempt was made to locate and recover impacted bullet fragments within the castle grounds using three 2m² test pits and removing 10cm spits of soil to detect and re-detect the location of objects for three-dimensional positional recording. Unfortunately, the terms of the permission granted to excavate within the area of the scheduled monument limited excavation to the topsoil only, and prohibited any exploration passing through layers of stratigraphy. Each test pit promptly encountered a demolition layer post-dating the siege no deeper than 30cm from the turf layer, thus preventing recovery of objects other than modern detritus resulting from tourist activity.

Interpretation and future research questions

Despite the strength of the evidence for the location of the defences at the edge of the former garden platform, as well as it being the most logical approach for fortification from a point of practicality, the position of the defences requires further archaeological exploration before the hypothesis above can be properly tested. Reassessment of the bullet evidence from this area using data gathered in recent ballistic terrain-impact studies may begin to identify a signature for bullets that struck the earthworks.[29] However geophysical survey and a trial excavation would be the best approach to ascertain whether the outline of their position can by identified through the soil disturbance caused by modern ploughing. This may also be possible within the castle grounds to the immediate north-west of the fortified site; however the area to the west is most likely entirely lost due to later development by the Castle Farm site.

The high proportion of pistol and carbine calibre bullets in the recovered assemblage, together with a low quantity of larger musket calibres may reflect several possibilities. It is likely that a significant number of the soldiers of the garrison were drawn from Vincent Corbet's dragoon regiment, possibly even a single company as hinted by the array of officers, soldiers, colours and supplies captured in the action. That being the case, a higher proportion of carbine and pistol calibres would be expected amongst the defensive fire by the garrison. The multitude of pistol shot may represent officers and dragoons using weapons to hand as well as be an indication of the proximity of the Parliamentarian soldiers at the point of engagement, as both accounts indicate that the attackers got to within a very short distance of the defences before the alarm was raised.

---

29 Colin J. Parkman, *Experimental Firing, and Analysis of Impacted 17th–18th Century Lead Bullets* (University of Huddersfield, 2017), Doctoral Thesis.

The apparent correlation between densities of bullets in the landscape with those areas of small-arms impact scar density on the surrounding structures, would suggest that it is indeed possible to identify the locations of distinct groups during the action within the landscape. Given the potentially large scale of the defensive circuit and the relatively small garrison left after Corbet's departure to Montgomery, this clustering hints at the defenders dividing into reactionary groups to best counter specific teams of attacking soldiers in the landscape, as well as possibly showing the division of the attackers as they aimed to draw the attention of the garrison from a small assault party. The impact scars would also seem to indicate that little or no fire was given to the windows of the castle as per Vicars's account. There is no evidence of stray impacts occurring on the frames or sills of the surviving windows, and the scars that have been identified on the castle occur at a range of heights that would support the indication of targets in positions outside of the building.

The projected origin of the impacts on the southern wall are particularly tantalising evidence that the assault itself may well have come into the defences from the south and moved through the gardens before entering the castle through one of the two small doorways on the southern face of the Elizabethan range. This seems a counterintuitive point of attack, as it requires the most defended ground to be covered to reach the castle from the projected location of the defences. With such a small garrison force in occupation this area would not have been practical to fully man during the early hours of the morning, when much of the garrison would likely have been asleep. Coupled with the prevalence of marshy ground to the south, and the likely direction of approach being from the nearest hostile garrison to the north-west, the relatively low threat of attack to this area of the defences may have left the sentry there unequipped to handle a direct assault. The small quantity of impact scars from attacking fire along the southern wall may also point to relatively few soldiers attacking this side of the castle, which would support the possibility that the assault party made their approach from the south of the castle while the mainstay of the attacking force occupied the defenders to the north and east.

Despite some survey activity to the west of the garden platform and in a single field to the north-west, the presence of scheduled monuments, permanent pasture, post-period development and a probable Victorian midden means that data collected here is less detailed and comprehensive than for the arable fields in the rest of the survey area. As such this prevents any conclusive analysis of the siege action from the artefact scatters alone, however the lack of more than a handful of possible impact scars on these faces of the castle would suggest that the fighting here was by no means as intense as on the eastern side of the site.

It is also unclear the degree, if any, to which the artefacts and impact scar evidence here overlap those of a prior engagement. More research is needed to identify evidence for the January-February 1644 siege and to help understand what influence it might have on the overall archaeological record. This problem may prove persistent for numerous siege locations where additional engagements occurred but were evidently too minor to be documented. Therefore, until this issue can be satisfactorily tackled, conclusions about the siege action drawn from the archaeology at Moreton Corbet will continue to carry an element of doubt.

Conclusions

Despite the small scale of the Moreton Corbet site and the siege action that took place there, its archaeological significance should not be underestimated. Sieges are still largely underrepresented in conflict archaeology studies for the Wars of the Three Kingdoms, despite the importance of garrisons to the campaigns of the civil wars in England,[30] and the greater number of recorded sieges in contrast to battles for those conflicts.[31] Due to the difficulties raised by the poor prospects for survival of the unstratified evidence at large-scale urban siege sites, small siege actions at rural garrisons may have to shoulder a greater share of the burden of future archaeological study of the evidence of fighting in siege actions.

The significance of impact scar evidence for the interpretation of historic engagements is only just beginning to be appreciated by the archaeological study of sieges. Further experimental research is undoubtedly required to unlock their potential to tell us about conflict in the past, particularly in terms of understanding what their cross-sectional profile might tell us about the shot that caused their formation, and developing an appropriate recording methodology to properly address that potential. Recording of scars with the best methodology available at this present stage of study however is preferable to their irrevocable loss. The necessity for a comprehensive recording programme of impact scars should not be understated, as impact scars are increasingly vulnerable to greater degrees of weathering due to environmental and pollution factors. In addition to this there is the pervasive threat from both restoration and developmental work on historic structure, and even during the course of the Moreton Corbet study, at least one impact scar on the church was irrevocably damaged during repointing work on the walls.

---

30   Peter Gaunt, *The English Civil War: A Military History* (London: I.B. Tauris & Co Ltd, 2014), pp.87–88.
31   Foard and Morris, *The Archaeology of English Battlefields*, pp.105–142.

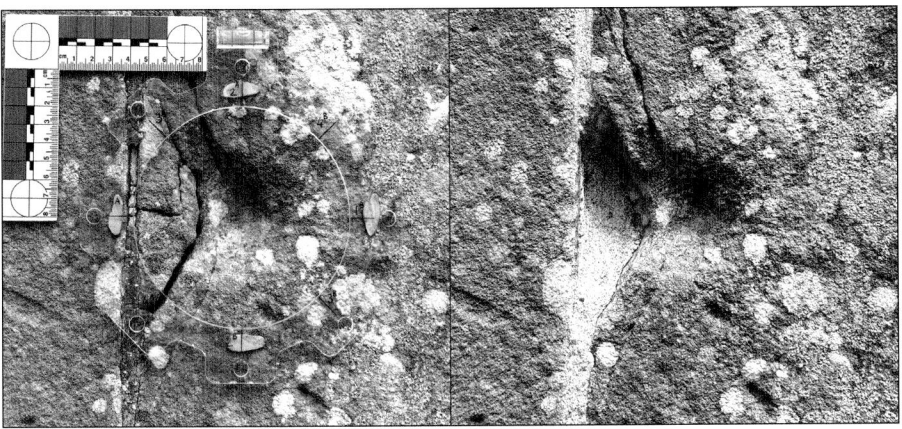

Scar C3 on St Bartholomew's Church. Left image taken during surveying in 2019 and right taken in 2022 after repointing work carried out in 2020. (Author's photo)

Greater awareness of their existence in local Historic Environment Records would potentially help avoid similar damage occurring elsewhere, though this too requires a comprehensive database of locations with impact scar evidence, something that does not yet exist. The establishment of a methodology to record and recover impacted bullet fragments that complement the impact scarring is also vital in this regard as a lack of awareness of what the archaeological signature looks like will prevent their proper protection from development, or their appropriate treatment in future excavation at sites with similar evidence.

Further work is yet required at Moreton Corbet to develop this early picture of the archaeology of the siege action, particularly in relation to the location of the fortifications. Further survey work would be advantageous to extend the coverage in the landscape to the south and the north in areas previously undetected, and a comparative study to examine the local degree of background noise for recreational shooting in later centuries would also help to identify the level to which the small calibre bullet skew in the survey results reflects the actual siege engagement.

Subsequent siegefield studies will undoubtedly require the evidence gathered by the Moreton Corbet study to be re-examined as the methodology is developed over time. Moreton Corbet nevertheless represents an important first step in the investigation and interpretation of a siege action through combining historic terrain reconstruction with the unstratified archaeology and impact scar evidence produced through attack and defence at an early modern garrison.

Bibliography

Border, Daniel, *The Weekly Account (Issue 56)* (London: Bernard Alsop, 1644)

Duffy, Christopher, *Siege Warfare: The Fortress in the Early Modern World 1494–1660* (London: Routledge, 1979)

Foard, Glenn, *Battlefield Archaeology of the English Civil War* (Oxford: BAR Publishing, 2012).

Foard, Glenn and Morris, Richard, *The Archaeology of English Battlefields: Conflict in the Pre-Industrial Landscape* (York: Council for British Archaeology, 2012)

Gaunt, Peter, *The English Civil War: A Military History* (London: I.B. Tauris & Co Ltd, 2014)

Harrington, Peter, 'Siegefields: An archaeological assessment of 'small' sieges of the British civil wars', *Journal of Conflict Archaeology*, 1 (2005), pp.93–113

Harwood, Elain, 'Moreton Corbet Castle', *English Heritage Historical Review*, 1 (2006), pp.37–40.

Parkman, Colin J., *Experimental Firing, and Analysis of Impacted 17th–18th Century Lead Bullets* (University of Huddersfield, 2017), Doctoral Thesis, <http://eprints.hud.ac.uk/id/eprint/34911>

Leese, Richard J., *Siege Archaeology of the English Civil Wars: Establishing a methodology to unlock the archaeology of attack and defence at early modern siege sites* (University of Huddersfield, 2020), Doctoral Thesis, <http://eprints.hud.ac.uk/id/eprint/35749>

Remfry, Paul M., *Moreton Corbet Castle, 1066 to 1700* (Worcester: SCS Publishing, 1999)

Vicars, John, *Magnalia Dei Anglicana* (London: J. Rothwell and T. Underhill, 1646)

Wilson-North, W. R., 'Formal Garden Earthworks at Moreton Corbet Castle, Shropshire', in M. Bowden, D. A. Mackay and P. Topping (eds.), *From Cornwall to Caithness: some aspects of British field archaeology. Papers presented to Norman V Quinnell* (BAR British Series 209, Oxford: BAR Publishing, 1989), pp.225–228

Worton, Jonathan, *To Settle the Crown: Waging Civil War in Shropshire 1642–1648* (Solihull: Helion & Company Ltd, 2016)

King's Lynn Under Siege

How a small field in North Lynn is changing our understanding of English Civil War fortress engineering

David Flintham

There was a predominance of siege-type actions over battles during the English Civil Wars: according to one recent study, in England there were eight sieges for every battle.[1] But this is not generally reflected by the majority of studies of the period, nor often enough, in the archaeology. Yet a siege, which might last days, weeks, or even months, leaves a potentially far greater archaeological 'footprint' than any battle, which typically would last just a few hours. So, to investigate an English Civil War siege has been the ambition of a group of archaeologists and historians for more than a decade. After some false starts elsewhere in the country, the King's Lynn under Siege (KLuS) community archaeology project was formed by the late Neil Faulkner and David Flintham in January 2018.[2]

KLuS is a long-term research, training, and education project based in the community combining historical and archaeological methods in the investigation of Civil War remains. Its specific aims include:

- Developing understanding of the extent, character, and purpose of the militarisation of King's Lynn during the English Civil War. This will also identify the techniques employed in constructing the town's defences, some of which KLuS consider unique and thus of national importance.

---

1   Glenn Foard and Richard Morris, *Archaeology of English Battlefields*, (York: Council for British Archaeology, 2012), pp.127, 175–9.
2   Had things turned out differently, the project might instead have been *Newark under Siege*, or *Bristol under Siege*.

- Exploring the relationship between contemporary military theory and the reality of improvised militarisation within the constraints of landscape, resources, and human ingenuity in practice.
- Exploring the human experience of soldiers and civilians during the siege through historical documents, the excavation of defences, camps, and contemporary settlements, and the recovery and analysis of artefact and ecofact assemblages.
- Educating schoolchildren, students, local volunteers, and the wider public in the history and experience of the Civil War through hands-on archaeology and a range of print, online, exhibition, and public-presentation opportunities.
- Publishing results in the following forms.
    a. full professional archive reports on all fieldwork within a year of completion.
    b. regular summary interims in the county journal.
    c. eventual full monograph publication of the project as a whole.
    d. regular popular publications in various formats accessible to a range of general audiences.

But why King's Lynn? Even now, histories of the Civil Wars still regard the Norfolk town and port of King's Lynn as something of a backwater to the wars, and its siege during the summer of 1643 as little more than a footnote. King's Lynn was never one of England's great walled medieval towns and wasn't surrounded by a circuit of masonry fortifications. This is despite the illusion created by Ordnance Survey maps which show the course of the defences by way of a dotted line marked with the caption Town Wall, leading locals to expect 'stone walls'.[3] Instead, the town's defences evolved organically: with the River Great Ouse protecting its western side, the rivers that flowed through the town were diverted to provide protection to the east, north, and south. Where there were gaps, earthen ramparts topped with wooden palisades were erected, and finally, to control passage in and out of the town, and also to collect taxes, gateways were erected, most notably on the London Road to the south and the Norwich road to the east. During the latter years of the Middle Ages, these gates were rebuilt in brick and stone (the South Gate is an impressive local landmark), and a short stretch of medieval masonry wall ran for 710m either side of the East Gate (damaged during the 1643 siege and finally demolished in 1800). Approximately 213m of the masonry wall is still

---

3   The impressive Saxon earthen ramparts surrounding Wareham are similarly captioned. I wonder if inhabitants of this Dorset town are under a similar illusion?

visible.⁴ Thus, the defences can be seen as being D-shaped, with the Great Ouse forming the straight side of the D.

Once an important Hanseatic League trading centre, by the reign of Henry VIII, (when the town was renamed from 'Bishops Lynn' to the secular, but regal, King's Lynn) its maritime importance had declined to the extent that it was not included in Henry's coastal defence programme, but new fortifications were constructed during the 1580s and 1620s. So, while no longer one of England's chief ports, it was still important to river and coastal shipping: nine counties could be reached by boat from King's Lynn, while its coastal craft sailed up and down the East coast of England, and across the North Sea, particularly to The Netherlands. During the 1520s, the town was ranked eighth, in the list of English towns by size and population, but by 1662, King's Lynn had declined to twenty-second.⁵ The population of the town during the 1640s would have been in the region of 7,500.⁶

At the outbreak of the English Civil War in 1642, like so many other towns up and down the country, the town's defences were repaired and improved. This is likely to have included the repair to gates, portcullises and drawbridges, and cleaning existing ditches that had become clogged over time. It was reported that during the summer of 1642, the town's Trained Bands were drilling, while in January 1643 the town was allowed to keep £400 from its subscription to Parliament to improve the town's fortifications.⁷ It is likely, that this improvement included the construction of a line of earthworks on the northern edge of the town, along the Fisher Fleet. However, such works were still inadequate, and in July 1643, Parliament authorised the re-fortifying of King's Lynn.⁸ But it was a scheme interrupted (if it ever actually commenced) by the siege and wouldn't recommence until the town was secured for Parliament.

---

4   Measurements from Hollar's *Groundplat of Kings Lyn* with Google Earth for visible remains.
5   Ranking is based on the Subsidy (1523–7), and Hearth Tax (1662), rankings exclude London. https://www.buildinghistory.org/town-rank.shtml (Accessed 30/12/2022)
6   It had increased from 6,000 in 1603 to 9,000 in 1670. John Patten, 'Population Distribution in Norfolk and Suffolk during the Sixteenth and Seventeenth Centuries', *Transactions of the Institute of British Geographers*, No.65 (London: The Royal Geographical Society with the Institute of British Geographers, 1975), p.49
7   *Journal of the House of Lords*: Volume 5, 1642–1643 (London, 1767–1830), pp.546–552. British History Online http://www.british-history.ac.uk/lords-jrnl [accessed 30 August 2022]
8   *Journal of the House of Lords*: Volume 6, 1643 under the date of 10 July 1643 (London, 1767–1830), pp.125–127. British History Online http://www.british-history.ac.uk/lords-jrnl [accessed 30 August 2022]

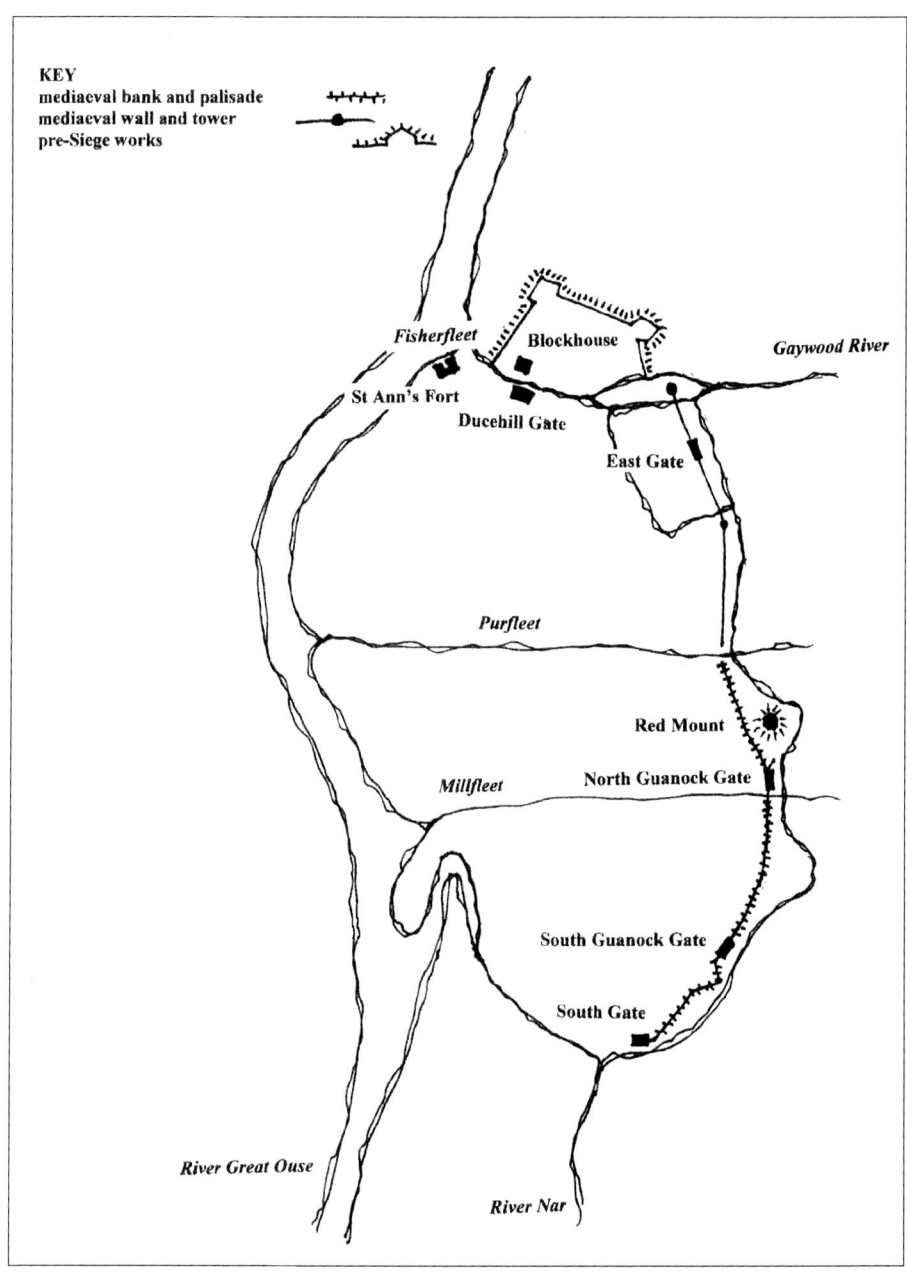

Plan of Kings Lynn at the 1643 Siege (after Mike Osborne)
King's Lynn's defences at the start of the siege were still largely reliant on water courses, especially to the south and west, and the medieval fortifications to the east. At the outbreak of the Civil Wars, a new line of fortifications was built to the north of the town. (With thanks to Michael Osborne. His original plan has been adapted to show only the defences that existed in early summer 1643)

In August 1643, with the Earl of Newcastle's Royalist army advancing south through Lincolnshire, a Royalist coup installed Sir Hamon L'Estrange as governor of King's Lynn. Parliament's reaction was swift, and a fleet under the Earl of Warwick was sent into the Wash to blockade the town from the sea, and the Earl of Manchester arrived before the town and assembled a force with which to besiege it. Blockaded, under bombardment, with its freshwater supplies disrupted, under the threat of assault, and with no relief in sight, on 16 September, King's Lynn surrendered.[9]

Parliament realised the importance of King's Lynn as a logistical hub. Raw materials, including Peak District lead[10] and local linseed, were brought into the town then shipped to London, while weapons and munitions were imported from abroad. All manner of supplies were brought into the town and then shipped on to Parliament's Army of the Eastern Association as it advanced through Lincolnshire and Yorkshire in 1643–4. The Siege of York in 1644 was supplied through King's Lynn, as was Cromwell's invasion of Scotland in 1650. But the King's Lynn merchants didn't always have things their own way, and Royalist privateers operating from Scarborough preyed on merchant ships; such was the nuisance of this that King's Lynn's merchants actually part-funded the Parliamentarian force sent to besiege Scarborough in 1645.[11]

Despite the improvements to the town's defences in 1642 and during the first half of 1643, at the time of the siege, King's Lynn's fortifications remained rather unsophisticated, and certainly bore little resemblance to those illustrated by Wenceslaus Hollar in his plan of *c.*1645. So, following the end of the siege, Richard Clampe,[12] a local physician and mathematician, was given the job of designing the new fortifications. Clampe had already designed the fort further upstream at Earith, and would later go on to design Parliament's siege works around Newark-on-Trent in 1645–6. His solution was for an enceinte to completely enclose the town on its north, east, and southern sides. It would include a fort at the town's South Gate, eight bastions, and two smaller works. The complete bastioned enceinte was approximately 4.36km in length.[13] Clampe's design was based on the latest Continental methods, utilising the principle of defence in depth, employing

---

9   The story of the siege and its importance to the overall history of the English Civil Wars is the subject of a forthcoming study by the author, and to be published by Helion & Co.
10 See David T. Kiernan, *The Derbyshire Lead Industry in the Sixteenth Century*, (Derby: Derbyshire Record Society, 1989), pp.95–7. The author is grateful to John Pigott, Hon. Recorder, Peak District Mines Historical Society for his advice on this topic.
11 David Cooke, *Yorkshire Sieges of the Civil Wars*, (Barnsley: Pen and Sword Family History, 2011), p.168
12 David Flintham, 'Richard Clampe, Fortress Engineer, *c.*1617–1696', *Fort*, number 46 (Fortress Study Group, 2019), pp.3–14.
13 Measurements based on Hollar's plan and, where features exist today, Google Earth.

multiple layers of ramparts, ditches, and moats, transforming the town into the strongest fortress in East Anglia.

At the outbreak of the English Civil War, King's Lynn's existing defences enclosed an area of approximately 129.7 hectares. The pre-siege earthworks to the north of the town enclosed an additional 13 hectares. But Clampe's bastioned enceinte enclosed an area of approximately 160.6 hectares, including the newly enclosed 15.5 hectares in the north, and 2 hectares in the south-west. The area inside the fortifications stretched 2.3km from north to south, and 1.1km from east to west.[14]

Held in the town's archive is Richard Clampe's scaled plan for the south-west bastion.[15] This plan is wonderfully detailed, using colour to set out the various components of the defences, as well as providing width measurements (in perches).

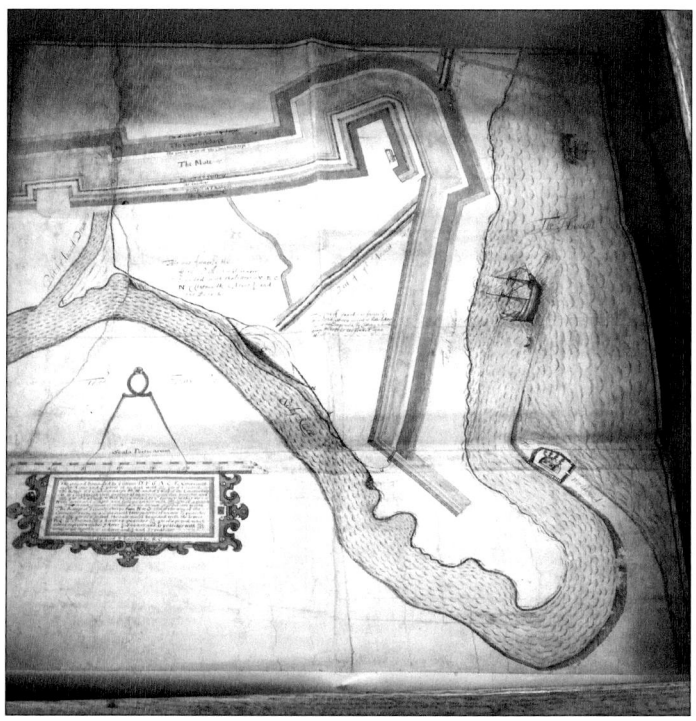

Richard Clampe's plan of King's Lynn's southern defences pictured on display in the Town's Archives. (Author's photograph)

14 All measurements are approximate and are based on Hollar's *Groundplat of Kings Lyn*.
15 Plan of the fortifications near the Boal, South Lynn, between Sechy River and the Haven. (NRO- King's Lynn Borough Archives, KL/C 48/16 (originally BC 21)) (With thanks to the Lynn Museum and King's Lynn Borough Archives)

This plan, combined with the typical height dimensions of English Civil War fortifications,[16] enabled the project to devise a scale profile of the fortifications.[17]

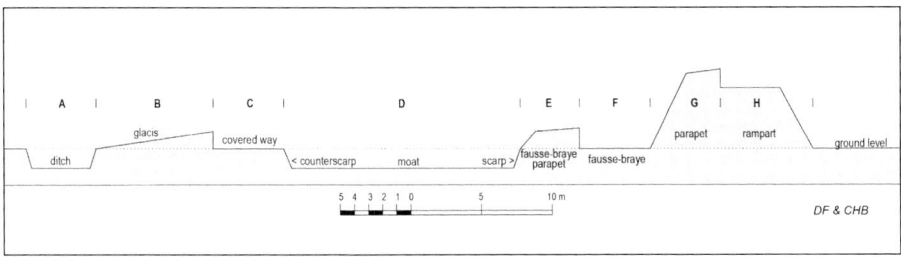

Profile of the fortifications drawn by Charles Blackwood and based on the author's analysis of Clampe's plan. (Thanks to Charles Blackwood, Fortress Study Group)

	Component	Width	Notes
A	Outer Ditch	5.029m	Clampe refers to this as the 'Ditch of counterscarp'
B	Glacis	8.381m	Clampe refers to this as the 'Counterscarp'
C	Covered Way	5.029m	
D	Moat	16.763m	
E	Parapet of Fausse-Braye	4.19m	Added together, the fausse-braye would have a total overall width of 9.219m
F	Fausse-Braye	5.029m	
G	Parapet	5.029m	Added together, the rampart would have a total overall width of 11.734m
H	Rampart	6.705m	
	Total	56.155m	

16 Based on the research of Lieutenant-Colonel W. G. Ross, R.E. in 'Military Engineering during the Great Civil War, 1642–9', in *Professional Papers of the Corps of Royal Engineers*, volume XIII (Chatham: Corps of Royal Engineers, 1887), plate I

17 The dimensions are taken from Clampe's plan of the south-west bastion and are scaled at 1 Perch = 5.029m. I am grateful to the artistic skills of Charles Blackwood of the Fortress Study Group for his help in developing this profile.

Clampe's plan demonstrates a level of sophistication seldom seen elsewhere during the English Civil Wars. Of the 157 towns in England thought to have been fortified during the English Civil Wars only Oxford and the design for Newport Pagnell come close to the level of sophistication found at King's Lynn.[18]

The existence of Clampe's plan focused the attention of KLuS on the site of the south-west bastion. But this is a feature that proves to be elusive: fieldwork undertaken in April 2019 followed by a magnetometry survey in May 2019 was inconclusive.

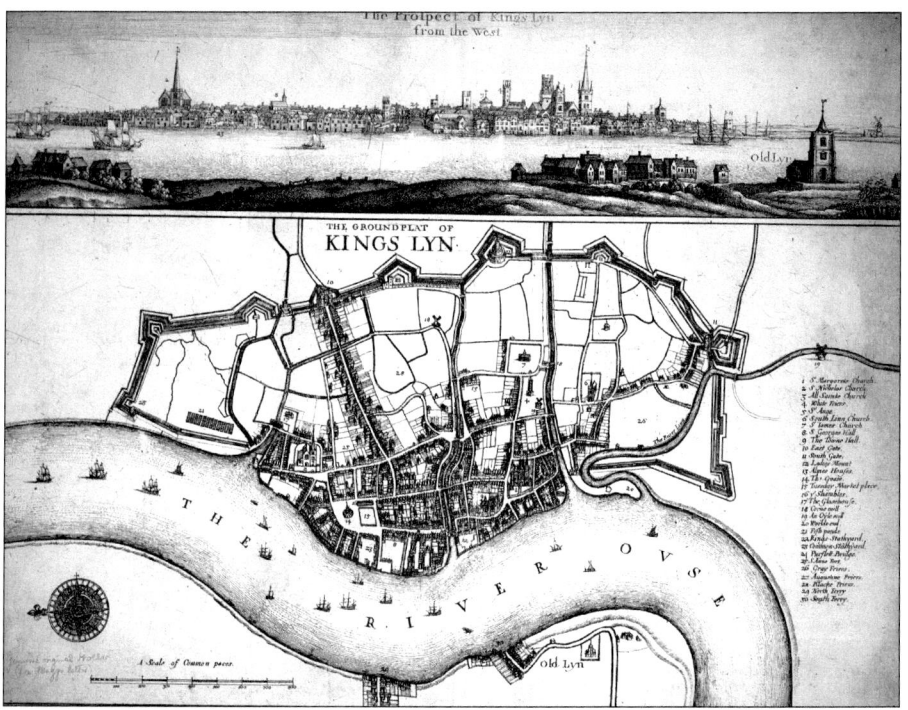

Wenceslaus Hollar's The Groundplat of Kings Lyn. This shows King's Lynn c.1645 when the refortification was complete. Despite several histories still claiming to the contrary, it does not portray the town at the time of the siege in August/September 1643.
(With thanks to The Thomas Fisher Rare Book Library, University of Toronto)

18 David Flintham, *The Town Well Fortified*, (Warwick: Helion and Company Limited), forthcoming.

Wenceslas Hollar's well-known *The Groundplat of Kings Lyn* (c.1645)[19] demonstrates the consistency of the layout of the fortifications, although it doesn't do as much justice to the actual complexity of their design. Hollar's plan would be the basis for the maps and plans that followed until the advent of the Ordnance Survey, including Henry Bell's *Groundplat of Kings Lyn* (1680), William Rastrick's *Iconographia* (1725), and the *Plan of the Town of Lynn* (1797). Hollar depicts the town as it appeared following the completion of Clampe's design, probably in 1645. Hollar's precise activity between 1643 and his arrival in Antwerp in 1647 is unclear. He was in London in 1644 (he sketched the fort at Hyde Park in 1644), but any visit to King's Lynn is not documented.[20] However, what Hollar is certainly *not* depicting is the town at the siege in the summer of 1643, despite what several histories continue to claim.

It is the feature in the north-east corner of Hollar's plan that is of particular interest. Hollar is clearly depicting a multi-layered scheme of fortifications, most noticeably, the water-filled moat. To the south of the north-east bastion, the moat is still extant and is known today as the 'Long Pond' (although until recently, it was locally regarded as Victorian in origin). This feature narrows and continues northwards where it has become a water-filled ditch. Initial investigation in January 2020 identified the 'Pond' as the likely traces of the north-eastern bastion. This resulted in the project's attention to be focused there, and substantial desk-top research took place throughout 2020 and early 2021.

The project utilised a wide range of resources ranging from contemporary plans and descriptions, early maps, and more than a century's worth of Ordnance Survey maps. Google Earth and LiDAR technology were used as well. During this research, the project asked itself just what it wanted to achieve, and in particular six questions:

- Prove Clampe's plan: after all, "it's easy enough to draw an enormous earthwork from the comfort of your nice little town house, but how do we know that the people on the ground did not cut corners."[21]
- Understand the purpose, composition and construction of King's Lynn's earthwork fortifications.

---

19   *P987b Kings Lynn*, The Thomas Fisher Rare Book Library, University of Toronto
20   David Flintham, 'His Majestie's Scenographer: the Military Art of Wenceslaus Hollar, in *Home and Away: The British Experience of War, 1628–1721*, (Warwick: Helion and Company Limited, 2018), pp.174–5.
21   Dr Chole Duckworth, *The Great British Dig: History in Your Back Garden*, (London, Conway, 2022), p.211.

- What does the design and layout of the fortifications tell us about King's Lynn's topography as mapped by Wenceslas Hollar and subsequent maps?
- How were the fortifications armed and manned?
- What happened to the fortifications? How were they de-commissioned and removed?
- How do the lessons from King's Lynn translate nationally?

In spring 2021 plans were drawn up to undertake a non-intrusive investigation of the site. These plans were submitted to the Norfolk Historic Environment Record in April 2021.[22] Not long afterward, the project was contacted by Solstice Heritage, the archaeological consultants for Channel 4's *The Great British Dig* programme. During the spring and summer of 2021, KLuS worked closely with the programme, culminating in a five-day 'dig' in September 2021.[23] The project brought nearly four years of research to the programme, and this ensured that *The Great British Dig* trenches were positioned as accurately as possible. If the design planed by Richard Clampe nearly 380 years ago was proved to be accurate, then King's Lynn's fortifications would be the most sophisticated defences built anywhere during the British Isles during the 1640s.

During the dig, a trench measuring 30m x 1.8m and running approximately east to west was opened up in the field at the rear of Fairlawn House. While the report detailing the results of this excavation is yet to be published, there are three important findings to highlight: firstly, the moat in this part of the fortifications was wider than that illustrated in Clampe's plan for the south-western bastion (20m compared with 16.7m), the 'cuts' for the fausse-braye and main rampart matched almost exactly his plan,[24] and finally, the discovery of a wooden post and cross-piece at the (outer) base of the rampart suggests that the rampart was constructed using some sort of wooden framework. In addition to the main trench, *The Great British Dig* opened four smaller trenches including one to the east of the Long Pond which uncovered traces of the glacis.

---

22   Norfolk Historic Environment Record: ENF151503 (geophysical survey) and ENF151506 (field walking/ metal detecting).
23   Norfolk Historic Environment Record: ENF151929.
24   *The Great British Dig* excavation in September 2021 revealed the width of the moat to be 3.3m wider, so 20m wide. As all other widths match Clampe's plan, the total width of the fortifications at the north-east bastion is 59.32m

KING'S LYNN UNDER SIEGE 73

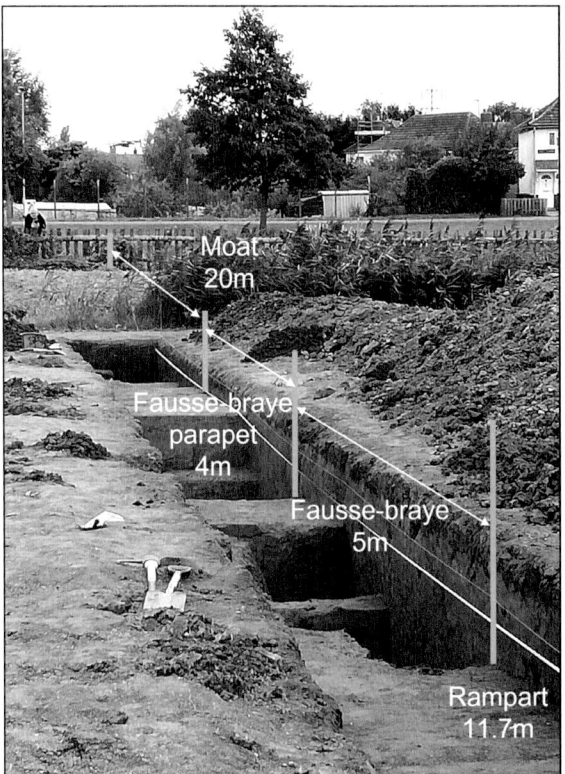

The main *Great British Dig* trench showing the 'cuts' from the various components of the fortifications. These proved to be very close to the profile developed from Clampe's plan. (Author's photograph)

A wooden post is revealed during *The Great British Dig* excavation in September 2021. Traces of a wooden cross-piece can be just seen at the base of the trench. Analysis suggested that this was part of the framework for the rampart, a theory corroborated by the discovery of a second post in 2022. (Author's photograph)

A number of people have commented that the King's Lynn episode was the best of the 2022 series of *The Great British Dig*: much of its success was down to it being able to tap into an existing project. That said, the programme was an enormous boost to KLuS. It generated considerable local (and wider) interest, and importantly, it enabled the project to establish a fantastic relationship with the owners of Fairlawn House, beneath whose fields lies much of the North-East bastion. The owners generously invited the project to return in 2022 (and in 2023 and 2024 as well).The project is fortunate that it is just a few miles to the south of Sedgeford, home of the Sedgeford Historical and Archaeological Research Project (SHARP), a community archaeology project founded by Neil Faulkner more than 25 years ago. Several members of the team had previous SHARP experience, and

Site overview (south at top)
An aerial view of the north-east bastion site during the 2022 excavation.
The shape and size of the bastion is clear.
a) is the approximate location of the main 2021 trench
b) is the 2022 trench
c) is the 'glacis' trench (2021)
d) is the 'Long Pond' – this is the best surviving part of Clampe's moat, although until our investigations, locals considered it to be of Victorian origin.
(Photograph with thanks to Gary Rossin)

thanks to Neil's involvement with both projects, it was decided to run the 2022 'season' under the SHARP umbrella. Tragically, Neil died at the beginning of 2022 and so was unable to see his dream of a Civil War siege project come to fruition.

A priority for the Project was to survey the entire site and on 25 March 2022, a magnetometry survey was undertaken. The results of this survey directed the planning for our 2022 season, particular in terms of where not to excavate.[25] The scale of the bastion can be best appreciated from the air, and at the end of the first week of the 2022 season a drone was able to take a number of aerial photographs. The first of these two images shows the bastion looking south. Of particular note is the existing stretch of moat (Long Pond). This extends further south than shown on this image, crossing Loke Road and still defines the shape of the Kettlemills bastion. Incidentally, the Kettlemills bastion marks the point where the northern extent of the fortifications extant at the 1643 siege connected to those constructed following the siege. The distance between the salient angle of the north-east bastion to the Kettlemills bastion (e.g., the distance that enfilading fire would cover) was 213m. According to Ross' analysis of Robert Ward's *Anima'dversions of Warre*, and Henry Hexham's translation of Marollois, the lines of defence (e.g., the distance between the salient angle of one bastion and the next) should not be greater than 219.45m (240 yards) for musketry defences, but could be greater for artillery defence.[26]

According to Ward, the moat (if wet) or ditch (if dry) should be 45.7m (50 yards) wide, while the fause-bray (an imported characteristic of the Flemish method of fortification according to Ross) was 4.57m–4.87m (15–16ft) from the foot of the rampart.[27] Finally, the face of the bastion should be 89.6m (98 yards). Our investigations found that the length of the eastern bastion face from the flank to the salient angle is approximately 60m. Unfortunately, it is not possible to measure the northern face since part of this has disappeared beneath subsequent development.

---

25 Sedgeford Historical and Archaeological Research Project, Archaeological Evaluation Report, March 2022, *Fluxgate Gradiometer Survey*, ENF151503 – North-East Bastion, King's Lynn

26 Ross, (1888), p.94.

27 Robert Ward's *Anima'dversions of Warre; Or, A Militarie Magazine of the Truest Rules, and Ablest Instructions, for the Managing of Warre, Etc...* (London: John Dawson, 1639); Ross, (1888), pp.94–5.

2021 and 2022 Rampart posts
A view of the 2022 trench looking roughly northwards. The two rampart posts are indicated. These are 3.35m (11ft) apart, interestingly, roughly the length of a ramrod for a larger cannon of the time. (Author's photograph)

While the 2021 investigation focused on proving the width of the fortifications, in 2022 the project concentrated on the line of the rampart, both in terms of finding more clues as to how the rampart was constructed, and also its actual thickness, although given the proven accuracy of Clampe's plan, there is little reason to doubt that it was in the region of 12m thick.

The project was also curious to learn more about what happened to the fortifications after the Civil Wars.

The 2022 season comprised two weeks: 17 to 22 July, and 24 to 29 July. There was a team of six during week one, and ultimately nine in week two. Due to the unprecedented high temperatures, plans were radically altered, and any thoughts of digging trenches by hand were quickly abandoned. A digger was employed (and even this overheated) to dig a single main trench. The line of the 2021 trench was revealed,[28] and a second rampart post was discovered, the distance between this and the one uncovered in 2021 was 3.35m (11ft). Both rampart posts were carefully

---

28 As of July 2022, the report from the 2021 'Great British Dig' had not been published and as a result, surveyed measurements were not available. So instead, we were reliant on my own notes (which proved to be surprisingly accurate).

examined, although it was agreed that neither would be lifted this time (although this might be something for a future visit). These and other features were carefully recorded: drawing, photography, and finds processing often providing welcome relief from the heat.

Drone view of trench at end of week 1
An aerial view of the trench at the end of week one of the 2022 season. The dotted line indicates the line of the rampart posts. (Photograph with thanks to Gary Rossin)

The site was discussed, including whether the rampart posts were actually some sort of marker posts used when the site was laid out prior to the construction of the fortifications. While this was plausible, the thickness of the posts, the likely cross-pieces, and the absence of similar posts marking out other features (such as the moat), suggests that this was unlikely, and so it is concluded that the posts were part of the fabric of the fortifications themselves.

Augering took place to sample the soil, and field walking was also undertaken (the finds from this were a mixture of pottery and clay-pipe stems, shells, and bits and pieces of brick and tiles). The first week was concluded by a drone survey of the site: as indicated previously, this revealed the layout of the bastion in all its glory. During week two, three test-pits were dug to 'chase' further rampart posts, and while we were unsuccessful in finding them, this exercise did provide some useful information about the overall site which will be valuable for future investigation.

Two of the project's younger volunteers looking at the eastern section of the trench in July 2022. Both are looking to study archaeology or history at university, so KLuS provides them with useful experience. (Author's photograph)

While this isn't a site that is rich in finds, we recorded 71 – including pottery, clay-pipe stems, some ironwork, and cockle and oyster shells. Most of the finds, particularly from the western half of the trench, related to the area's role as a brick-kiln at the end of the eighteenth century. We found several misfired bricks, charcoal, and clinker, all associated with this period in the site's history. However, the star find of the fortnight were two sizeable pieces of a later seventeenth century onion bottle, which hinted at the site's occupation after the wars, and also connects with the town's wine trade.

The most notable find from the dig were two pieces from a seventeenth century onion bottle, probable evidence of both the site's occupation after the Civil Wars, and the town's wine trade. Similar bottles have been recovered from the 1682 wreck of the *Gloucester*. (Author's photograph)

The discovery of two posts in alignment at the foot of the rampart suggest a method of construction of an English Civil War period rampart. A contemporary account recommends that a rampart of 'at least 11-foot-high and 23-foot thicke' would be required to provide adequate defence against cannon. But to construct six metres of artillery-proof earthworks 3.35m high and 7m deep would require the movement of in the region of 141.58 cubic metres of earth (more than 1,000 barrow loads).[29] Richard Norwood suggested that one man could dig 14.1 cubic metres per day, while Sir Richard Cave, a Royalist fortifications expert, estimated that 20 men could cast up some 12 metres of breastworks in 12 hours.[30]

Local geology would affect construction. In places earthwork ramparts were constructed on a base of gravel, while the type of soil encountered would impact

---

29 Stephen Bull, *The Furie of the Ordnance: Artillery in the English Civil Wars*, (Woodbridge: The Boydell Press, 2008), p.87.
30 Richard Norwood, *Fortification or Military Architecture*, (London: Andrew Crooke, 1639), p 123; J. Duncumb, *Collections towards the History and Antiquities of the County of Hereford*, volume 1 (Hereford: 1894), p.248.

on construction. The method of the construction of the ramparts would influence their design: without internal reinforcement a rampart would require a greater base-width and would be of a lesser height than a rampart that had a more solid foundation, a reinforced core and was revetted. Simply digging a ditch and putting the excavated soil behind would be insufficient to form a rampart strong enough or weatherproof.[31] So, with the site identified, the turf would be first stripped back, and put to one side for later use. Then the topsoil would be removed, and the foundations of the rampart laid.

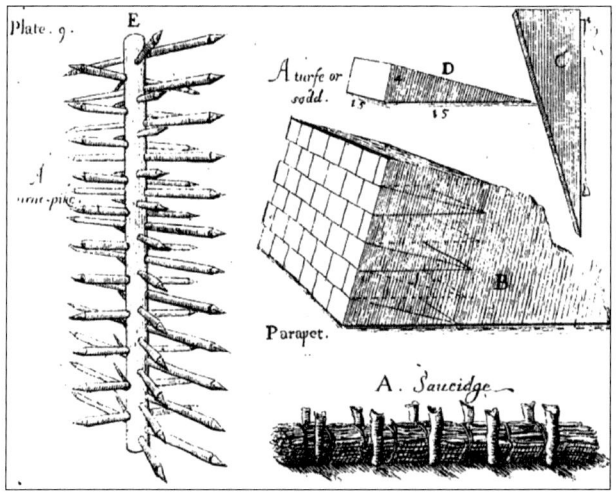

Plate 9 of Nicholas Stone's *Enchiridion of Fortification, Or A Handfull of Knowledge in Martiall Affaires* (1645) illustrating how turfs were to be cut, and then used to face ramparts. Also shown is the 'saucidge', something that may well have been used to construct a rampart. (Public Domain)

According to Nicholas Stone, the initial foundations of the rampart were secured by using a 'saucidge', which was a wooden stake of between 30.48–60.96cm (one and two feet) in height, tied together with 'brush wood'. Such foundations needed to be specifically secured near the ditch (moat). Stone wrote:

31 An intriguing (if perhaps over-engineered) method of earthwork construction in sixteenth century Siena is described in 'Simon Pepper and Nicolas Adams, *Firearms and Fortifications: Military Architecture and Siege Warfare in Sixteenth Century Siena*, (Chicago: The University of Chicago Press, 1986), p.74; see also John Harris, 'Karlovac: the Renaissance Ideal City in Central Europe', in *Fort*, volume 38, (Fortress Study Group, 2010), p.66.

> First you must drive stakes of a competent length, and at a reasonable distance, as you Saucidges, either for their greatness, or smallness shall require. Either one foot high, 1 foot and ½, or sometimes two foot in height.
>
> Then between these stakes you must depress bundles of small brush wood, bound fast together: Filling them in the midst with brick-bats, if you would sinke them in a River, but with earth, if you intend them a foundation in a Moat all along the said Work.[32]

The evidence from 2021 and 2022 along with what can be learned from the contemporary accounts suggests a method of construction where the rampart would be formed from stepped layers of hammered clay, supported by the wooden stakes. Ensuring that the height and depth of each step are equal will result in the desired 45 degree angle for the rampart. With the stakes and cross-pieces in place, the ditch would be excavated, and a layer of the excavated earth piled behind the wood. This would be hammered firm. On top of this layer, and slightly further back, a second row of stakes and cross-pieces would be inserted. More earth would be piled against this, and again rammed firm. Subsequent stepped layers of hammered earth, each supported by stakes and wood/brushwood would be added until the desired height of the rampart had been achieved.

The original turf was then used to face the rampart, providing additional strength and protection. According to Norwood, the individual pieces should be 12.7cm (4–5 inches) wide and 38.1cm (14–15 inches) in length and shaped 'like a wedge'. This wedge is cut in a triangular shape so that the rampart achieves its slope.[33] As a result of the need for turf, local pastureland would be stripped, rendering it unusable, much to the chagrin of local farmers. At the top of the rampart, a parapet, perhaps constructed from gabions, would be added. Finally, while an average sized rampart could keep cavalry out, determined infantry could scale ramparts relatively easily, and as a result, ramparts would also include additional defensive measures including wooden palisades and sharpened storm-poles.

While there won't be any evidence for the 'steps' above the base as these were lost during the brick-making phase of the site, nevertheless, this is a very plausible theory, and this method of rampart construction needs to be proven through experimental archaeology (the reconstruction of a section of ditch-fronted rampart is planned, probably for 2024).

As is always the way with archaeology, the excavations in 2021 and 2022 answered a number of questions, but raised a number more; questions which will

---

32　Nicholas Stone, *Enchiridion of Fortification*, (London: Richard Royston, 1645), p.34
33　Norwood, (1639), p.93; Stone, (1645), p.35

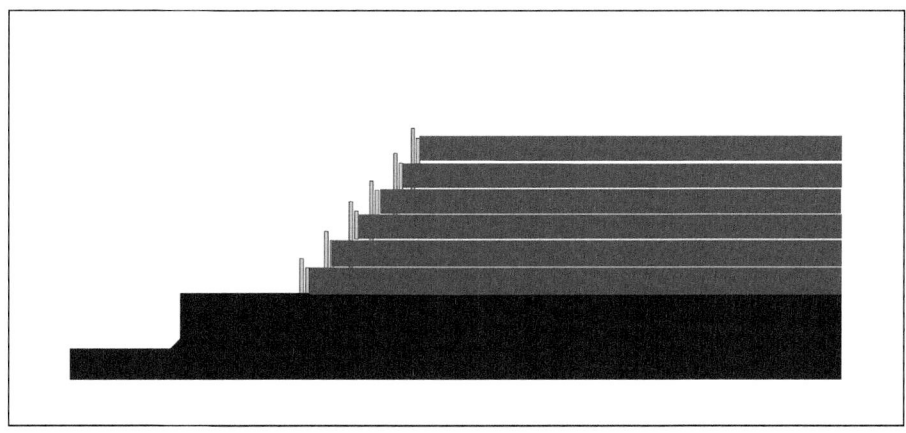

Rampart Reconstruction Profile
Findings from the project have demonstrated how English Civil War period ramparts may have been constructed: this method is based on 'steps' of hammered clay supported by posts such as those uncovered in 2021 and 2022.

be the objectives for future seasons. This research demonstrated the consistency between Clampe's plan and subsequent maps of the town, and that his plan for the south-west bastion was repeated in at least one other location, and probably around the entire circuit. As a result, any suspicion that his plan was little more than a theory invented from the comfort of his town house, have been firmly laid to rest.

The reason the fortifications extended so far to the north of the town, encompassing a wide expanse of open ground is explained by *Iconographia* (William Rastrick's 1725 plan of Kings Lynn) which illustrates livestock grazing in this area. Horse and oxen were vital for moving artillery and transporting munitions and supplies, and their loss could seriously limit the conduct of a campaign. The project has also shown that the fortifications were not removed following the end of the Civil War, and more than 70 years later, Daniel Defoe noted how strong the fortifications still were.[34] Instead, the fortifications, albeit overgrown and weathered, lasted until the end of the eighteenth century when realising that a huge amount of standing mature clay existed around the town, the clay from the fortifications was harvested to make bricks (mature clay makes better bricks than new clay). William Faden's 1797 *Plan of the Town of Lynn*[35] shows

---

34   Pat Rogers (editor), Daniel Defoe, *A Tour through the Whole Island of Great Britain*, (London: Penguin Books, 1986), p.97.
35   William Faden, *Plan of the Town of Lynn* from *Norfolk in six sheets* (1797)

the existence of brick kilns in two of the town's bastions, and the 2022 dig found evidence that brick making did actually take place on site. Faden's map was the last to show the fortifications as existing features, and by the time of John Wood's 1830 plan,[36] and the Ordnance Survey map of 1832, King's Lynn's fortifications, with the exception of the Red Mount (then known as *Lady's Mount*) had mostly disappeared.

Regardless of its television 'stardom', King's Lynn under Siege is very much a community project. In addition to the archaeology, the project is a significant educator, presenting talk and tours to a variety of groups. During the July 2023 fortnight we welcomed a number of visitors including town councillors, friends

Civil War Siege Shuffle KLuS is very much part of the Town's heritage community. During 2022 we supported a team of young historians who, through a local museum, devised a card game based on the siege of King's Lynn. Generously, the KLuS logo features prominently. (Author's photograph)

---

36   King's Lynn Record Office, KL/SE 3/18 – *Plan of King's Lynn Engraved plan by John Wood, 1830, showing...*

of the landowners, local authors, town guides, members of the Battlefields Trust, and the King's Lynn and West Norfolk Archaeological Society, and True's Yard, Stories of Lynn, the Lynn Museum, and the Cromwell Museum. Engaging with the public is a vital part of any community archaeological project and should never be undervalued. The project has also supported the development of the Civil War Siege Shuffle card game devised by King's Lynn's *Time Turners* youth project, and since 2022, the project has been asked to speak at events run by a number of organisations and societies. In addition, a number of magazines (such as *Current Archaeology*) and the journals of renowned societies have also covered the work of the project. KLuS is indeed fortunate to have found its home in King's Lynn, and is now well established in the local heritage community. Thanks go to everyone involved in the project, especially the landowners, the SHARP, and the 2021, 2022, and 2023 teams.

Looking ahead, the excavations to date have uncovered the fortifications running south to north, but somewhere close to the 2022 trench, these turned westwards. This itself presents a further question: given the 60m width of the fortifications, the 90 degree turn where the south–north course of the fortifications turns to run east–west would have occupied a large area. Unfortunately, there simply was not the time (nor, it should be said, the weather) to explore this in 2022, so this would be the priority for any further investigation of the site. During July 2023, soil samples of the entire site were taken and the results of this will inform the plans for the 2024 season.

King's Lynn has an extensive Town Archive, although because of the pandemic, it was closed until July 2022. In addition, recent discoveries in the National Archives include a set of accounts for payments to the gunners based in King's Lynn between January and March 1644, which importantly names nine of the town's forts and bastions, including one, protecting the town's western approaches, which was completely unknown until now. A further document suggests that the fortifications were constructed between November 1643 and May 1644.[37] The project is in the process of analysing these documents.

There is one further known plan by Clampe: a sketch plan of the fortifications and bastion located at Kettlemills, which is the next bastion from the North East bastion (going south). This is the point where the post-siege fortifications connected to those constructed prior to the siege. This is an area deserving of further investigation, while examination of the construction of the town's masonry walls has commenced, and for comparison purposes, an examination of the Red Mount bastion (the best-known feature of the town's defences) is also required.

---

37 TNA, SP28/238, f.2r, SP28/222 f.447r, 529r, 584r. With thanks to Simon Marsh for bring this to my attention.

Red Mount Bastion looking NW
The Red Mount bastion is the best preserved and most well-known feature of the town's earthwork defences. (Author's photograph)

Despite its name, the project's focus to date has very much been on how King's Lynn was fortified in the aftermath of the siege, rather than the siege itself. Therefore, the project will also be looking for evidence of the siege: in particular, the site of one of the siege batteries opposite the town is being sought: nearly 60 years ago what is thought to be part of a cannon dating from the siege was discovered close by, so is an obvious candidate for further investigation.

When considered alongside the siege of Gloucester which was happening more of less simultaneously, the siege of King's Lynn in August and September 1643 should be seen as a turning point of the Civil Wars. There is also some justification in regarding the siege as the birthplace of the Army of the Eastern Association; while in existence prior to the siege, it was the army that the Earl of Manchester formed outside the walls of the town during the summer of 1643 that would become Parliament's most effective fighting force until the advent of the New Model Army.

Writing in the 1880s, Ross considered that there was not a complete example of the Dutch method of fortification in England. He felt that Oxford was the nearest,[38] but what we have discovered means that King's Lynn comes even closer. Finally, the project's discoveries, particularly in respect of the design and construction of earthwork fortifications are very much 'of national importance'.

For more information, e-mail the project at kingslynnundersiege@outlook.com

Bibliography

Primary Sources
Archive
The National Archives
SP28/238, f.2r
SP28/222 f.447r, 529r, 584r

Norfolk Record Office - King's Lynn Archive
KL/C 48/16 (originally BC 21)
KL/SE 3/18

House of Lords Journal, (London, 1767-1830), Volumes 5 and 6

Printed
Norwood, Richard, *Fortification or Military Architecture*, (London: Andrew Crooke, 1639)
Stone, Nicholas, *Enchiridion of Fortification*, (London: Richard Royston, 1645)
Ward, Robert, *Anima'dversions of Warre; Or, A Militarie Magazine of the Truest Rules, and Ablest Instructions, for the Managing of Warre, Etc…*, (London: John Dawson, 1639)

Secondary Sources

Published
Bull, Stephen, *The Furie of the Ordnance: Artillery in the English Civil Wars*, (Woodbridge: The Boydell Press, 2008)
Cooke, David, *Yorkshire Sieges of the Civil Wars*, (Barnsley: Pen and Sword, 2011)
Duckworth, Chole, *The Great British Dig: History in Your Back Garden*, (London, Conway, 2022)
Duncumb, J., *Collections towards the History and Antiquities of the County of Hereford*, (Hereford: 1894), volume 1

---

38   Ross, (1888), p.95.

Flintham, David, 'His Majestie's Scenographer: the Military Art of Wenceslaus Hollar in *Home and Away: The British Experience of War, 1628-1721*, (Warwick: Helion and Co, 2018)

Flintham, David, 'Richard Clampe, Fortress Engineer, c1617-1696' in *Fort*, (Fortress Study Group, 2019), number 46

Flintham, David, *The Town Well Fortified*, (Warwick: Helion and Company, forthcoming)

Foard, Glenn, and Morris, Richard, *Archaeology of English Battlefields*, (York: Council for British Archaeology, 2012)

Harris, John, 'Karlovac: the Renaissance Ideal City in Central Europe' in *Fort*, (Fortress Study Group, 2010), number 38

Kiernan, David T., *The Derbyshire Lead Industry in the Sixteenth Century*, (Derby: Derbyshire Record Society, 1989)

Pepper, Simon, and Adams, Nicolas, *Firearms and Fortifications: Military Architecture and Siege Warfare in Sixteenth Century Siena*, (Chicago: The University of Chicago Press, 1986)

Rogers, Pat, (editor), *Daniel Defoe, A Tour through the Whole Island of Great Britain*, (London: Penguin Books, 1986)

Ross, Lieutenant-Colonel W. G. Ross, R.E., 'Military Engineering during the Great Civil War, 1642-9', *Professional Papers of the Corps of Royal Engineers*, (Chatham: Corps of Royal Engineers, 1887)

Maps and Plans

Faden, William, Plan of the Town of Lynn from Norfolk in six sheets (1797)

Hollar, Wenceslas, P987b Kings Lynn, (The Thomas Fisher Rare Book Library, University of Toronto)

Reports

Norfolk Historic Environment Record

ENF151503

ENF151506

ENF151929

Archaeological Evaluation Report, March 2022, Fluxgate Gradiometer Survey, ENF151503 – North East Bastion, King's Lynn (Sedgeford Historical and Archaeological Research Project, 2022)

Websites

https://www.buildinghistory.org/town-rank.shtml

Newark in the Civil Wars

Kevin Winter

During the English Civil Wars Fortresses Symposium, held in Newark on 19 November 2022, I led a tour of some of the Civil War related sites in the town. This chapter will examine why Newark became known as the 'Key to the North' and how the earthwork fortifications developed.

On 22 August 1642 King Charles I raised his standard at Nottingham Castle, effectively marking the beginning of the Civil Wars. By raising his standard in the middle of the country Charles hoped that support would come from far and wide. The reality was that little support showed up, however it was remarked that one town showed great support, with seven regiments raised in support of the King. That town was Newark, which would remain staunchly Royalist throughout the First Civil War (1642–1646). Why was Newark such a hotbed of Royalist support and how did it become known as the 'Key to the North'?

To answer these questions we need to go back several hundred years. When Bishop Alexander 'The Magnificent' was given permission by Henry I to build a stone castle at Newark in 1135, the Bishop was also given permission to build a bridge over what was probably then just a ford across the River Trent. This resulted in the Great North Road being diverted from the Roman Ermine Street, which led to a ferry across the River Humber in North Lincolnshire, through Newark and via Doncaster to York, thereby avoiding the ferry crossing. Newark became the crossing point of the Fosse Way, from Exeter to Lincoln, and the Great North Road, and the last crossing place of the Trent eastwards before it became tidal. The situation of the town and castle on a river gravel terrace, guarding these crossing places, gave the town a strategic significance, such that during the First Civil War it became known as the 'Key to the North'.

At Henry VIII's death, in 1547, he was succeeded by his 9 year old son Edward. Edward VI continued with his father's reformation of the church, and at the beginning of his reign the Bishop of Lincoln gave the castle and manor of Newark to the Crown. It remained in Crown hands until the Civil Wars. Therefore, many local landowners paid their rents to the Crown, thus when it came to taking sides it was natural for them to support their landlord.

In 1642 the castle was owned by the Queen, Henrietta Maria, Charles I's wife. In addition the Stuart monarchs were frequent visitors to Newark. Charles I's father, James I, travelled south from Scotland in 1603 along the Great North Road on his way to London to take the Crown following the death of Elizabeth I. He stopped off at Newark on his way and on other occasions when travelling the Great North Road. Charles I was also a frequent visitor and was in Newark in July of 1642, before raising his standard at Nottingham. There is a chalice in the Treasury at St Mary Magdalene Church in the town that was used by Charles I during his visits. That familiarity may also have played a part in the people's support for the Royalist cause.

It might be thought that support for the King would only come from the landowning class, but this doesn't appear to be the case. We are lucky to have an eyewitness account of some of the events of the Civil War in Newark in the diary of John Twentyman, landlord of the *Saracen's Head Inn* on the Market Place.[1] When the regiments raised for the King were away on the Edgehill campaign in autumn 1642, Parliamentarians from Lincoln saw their chance and tried to take the town for Parliament. Twentyman tells us that a drum was found in a cupboard and the towns' people came out, armed with scythes and pitchforks to beat off the Parliamentarian force. In December 1642 the Royalists decided to garrison the town and the first of four military governors was appointed, John Henderson. Henderson was a Scot, who had learned the art of warfare during the Thirty Years' War in the Low Countries, where many of the Civil War commanders on both sides had cut their teeth.

First Siege

When Henderson took office, the town had expanded beyond the medieval town walls along Slaughterhouse Lane and Lombard Street and a low ditch was dug as a crude defence. Twentyman tells us that it was so shallow that a man could easily leap across it. The first siege took place on 27–28 February 1643, when 6,000 Parliamentarians led by Major General Thomas Ballard surrounded the town. On 28 February Henderson placed his men in barns either side of Barnby Gate. As the Parliamentarians attacked along Barnby Gate they were repulsed. As evening fell on the other side of town, Henderson sensed that the Parliamentarians stationed along North Gate were tiring and led a mounted attack against them.

---

1 Nottingham University Manuscripts Department (hereafter NUMD), Mellish Papers, Twentyman Manuscript, Me Lm 1.

Ballard and his 6,000 men soon surrendered, far too easily for some of the national Parliamentarian leaders, who questioned Ballard, who was not given another military command.

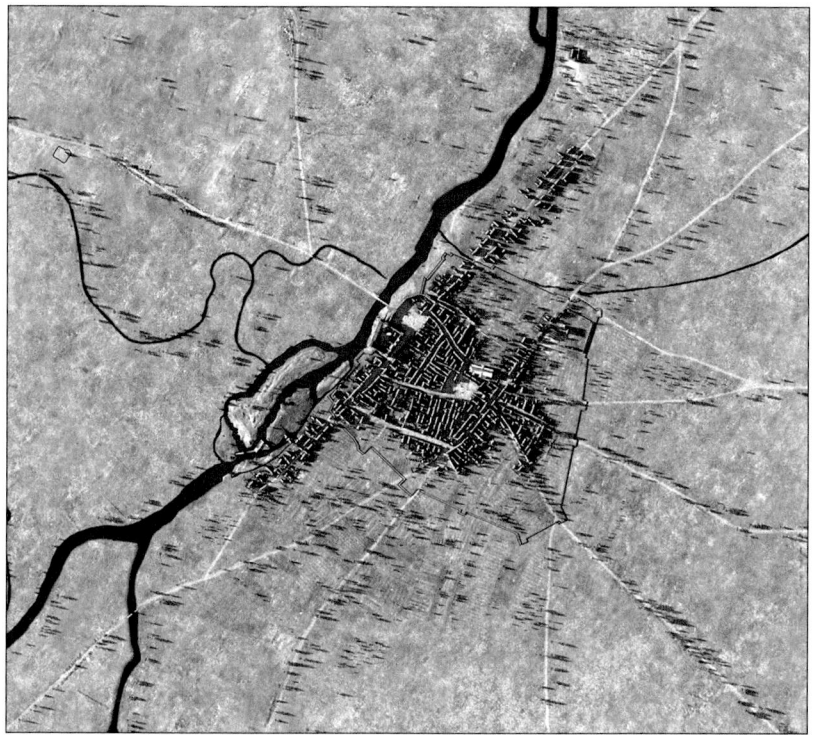

Town defences at the time of the first siege – map by Stuart Fleming. (Courtesy of the National Civil War Centre, Newark Museum – NCWC)

Henrietta Maria's Visit

Before the Civil War broke out the Queen had been sent to the Continent to help raise troops and to buy arms and armour for her husband's forces. She arrived at Bridlington in February 1643, with a mercenary army around 2,500 strong. After spending some time in York she made her way south, arriving in Newark on 16 June. She was hosted by Lord and Lady Frances Leeke, who rented the castle from her and owned a number of former church properties, including the Friary,

Chauntry House and the timber framed buildings on Kirk Gate, which has a plaque stating that this may have been where she was housed during her visit. It is now thought that this would not have been grand enough for the Queen, but some of her household may have stayed there. It is possible that she may have stayed in the Governor's House on Stodman Street.

The Governor's House, Stodman Street, Newark. (Courtesy of NCWC)

During the time the Queen was in Newark an attack was launched on Parliamentarian Nottingham. This was led by Baron Christoph von Dohna, a Bohemian mercenary commander, who was leading the attack from a boat on the Trent, when he was cut in two by a Parliamentary cannonball. His body was returned to Newark and he was interred in the crypt of St Mary Magdalene. In 1883 when the crypt was being prepared as the Treasury, his body, along with another 30, was removed and buried in the church gardens. Today a plaque marks the spot.

Henderson Replaced as Governor

Despite some initial successes, failures later in the year, most notably the Battle of Winceby on 11 October 1643, led to Henderson being replaced as Governor by Sir Richard Byron. Byron was one of seven brothers, whose family home was at Newstead Abbey. His older brother, John, was in charge of Royalist forces in the North-West. Byron had time to strengthen the defences before the next siege began.

Second Siege

On 29 February 1644, 7,000 Parliamentarians, led by Sir John Meldrum, surrounded the town. They took the bridges leading onto 'the Island' at Kelham and Muskham and established a bridge of boats, somewhere along North Gate in the vicinity of the Spital. This time they had a number of cannon and mortars, with which they could bombard the town. One of these was a 32pdr Demi-Cannon, known as 'Sweet Lips', supposedly named after a Hull prostitute. Given its size and the state of the roads it was floated down the river from Hull on barges. A battery was set up on Beacon Hill and the town was bombarded most nights between midnight and one in the morning. The *Olde White Hart* was hit and damaged, as was the church spire, which was probably being used as a lookout – the hole (or a replacement?) can still be seen today from Mount Walk. It is likely that the target for the Parliamentarians was the Governor's House. Across the road, on the corner of the Market Place stood the home of Hercules Clay, an Alderman and later Mayor of the town. Clay dreamt three times that his house would be destroyed by a Parliamentarian grenado (a ceramic shell filled with flammable materials, designed to set fire to the thatched roofs). Following the third dream Clay decided to move his family out and, sure enough, on 11 March his house was destroyed by a grenado. In recognition of God's part in his salvation Clay left a legacy of £100 for a memorial service to be held annually on the Sunday closest to 11 March. A tradition that still takes place today. He also gave £100 to be used to buy penny loaves for the poor. This money was used initially to strengthen the defences, but was later used for its intended purpose. Clay was a mercer (cloth merchant) and the annual service now commemorates the business community in the town, with bread rolls given to homeless charities. A plaque on the National Westminster Bank marks the spot where his house once stood and there is also a plaque commemorating his bequest in St Mary Magdalene. Just across Stodman Street from the Bank is the Governor's House, which was probably the intended target.

Town defences at the time of the second siege – map by Stuart Fleming. (courtesy of NCWC)

Rupert's Relief

Prince Rupert, Charles I's nephew, was campaigning in the North-West around Chester on 12 March when he received orders from his uncle to relieve the siege of Newark. By 15 March he was at Bridgnorth in Shropshire, and on 18 March he rendezvoused with Lord Loughborough at the latter's headquarters at Ashby-de-la-Zouch. Two days later he was at Bingham. Circling around the besieging forces, by dawn on 21 March his advance guard were established on the upper slopes of Beacon Hill. As dawn broke he led a series of charges against the Parliamentarians, eventually pinning them back against their bridge of boats. At a signal from Rupert, Byron led the defenders of Newark across the Town Bridge to take the bridges at Muskham and Kelham, before circling back behind the

Parliamentarians. Meldrum was forced to surrender. The Parliamentarians were allowed to march away, but had to surrender their weapons. Over 3,000 muskets, 11 artillery pieces, including 'Sweet Lips', and 2 mortars were surrendered. The relief of Newark is thought by some to be Prince Rupert's most brilliant military victory. Having returned the troops he 'borrowed' for the relief to their garrisons Rupert marched back to Shrewsbury.

Strengthening the Defences[2]

Although the defences had been strengthened before the second siege they were strengthened further following it. There is a possibility that they were designed by Sir Bernard de Gomme, the King's chief engineer, who had accompanied Prince Rupert during the relief of Newark from the second siege. A 1646 map of the defences and besiegers' earthworks as they were at the end of the final siege, drawn on vellum, is displayed at the National Civil War Centre Newark Museum. Handwriting comparisons have been carried out with examples of de Gomme's handwriting but were inconclusive.

The earthwork defences were built up around the town, with a 'porte' or gate constructed on Millgate, Balderton Gate and North Gate, with inner and outer

Royalist siege map showing the defences around the town and the besiegers earthworks. Unfinished drawing on Vellum. Courtesy of NCWC.

2   A survey of the surviving siege works was undertaken in the early 1960s, see Royal Commission on Historical Monuments, *Newark-on-Trent: The Civil War Siegeworks* (London: HMSO, 1964).

gates giving access into the town. Petitions in the Borough Minutes[3] record house owners claiming compensation for their demolished houses on both Millgate and North Gate. Outside the town large star shaped sconces were built. The Queen's Sconce was built alongside the Fosse Way and commanded the confluence of the Rivers Devon and Trent. On the other side of town the King's Sconce was built on top of the remains of what had once been St Leonard's Hospital, or the Spital, established by Alexander 'the Magnificent' in the twelfth century. By the time of the Civil Wars it had become Exeter House, owned by the Marquess of Exeter. The Parliamentarians had used it during the first siege as cover from which to fire into the town. Although partly demolished, it was used as cover again during the second siege. It was demolished, along with any dwellings outside the walls along North Gate, and the King's Sconce built on its site. John Twentyman's diary[4] tells us that Captain Edward Twentyman and the town's regiments helped in the construction of the earthworks. A cannon could be placed in each corner of the sconces, which had a garrison of around 150 men. The Queen's Sconce was surrounded by 'pitfalls' – pits dug with a sharpened stake hammered into the bottom of them, then loosely covered over; anyone treading onto them would be likely to get a nasty surprise! Although the King's Sconce fell victim to the towns industrial expansion along North Gate, its name survives in some of the street names of the new estate by the side of the river. There were also sconces at Muskham Bridge and on the 'island' protecting the approaches to the town.

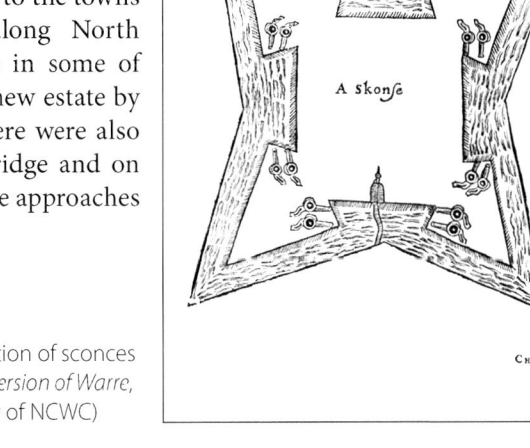

Instructions on the construction of sconces from Robert Wards *Animadversion of Warre*, (London: 1639). (courtesy of NCWC)

3   Nottinghamshire Archives, DC/NW/3/1/1, Newark Borough Corporation Minutes (hereafter Borough Minutes).
4   NUMD, Mellish Papers, Twentyman Manuscript, Me Lm 1.

Aerial view looking west north west of the Queen's Sconce. Photographer Ian Bracegirdle, (courtesy of NCWC)

The Final Siege

Charles and Rupert's Quarrel

In October 1644 Sir Richard Byron was replaced as Governor by Sir Richard Willys. After the Battle of Marston Moor on 2 July 1644, things had begun to go badly for the Royalists. As they lost control of the north, Newark became less strategically important but became a mustering place for Royalist support. It is thought that the population of Newark, which was around 2.300[5] at the beginning of the Civil War, probably increased by a factor of three due to the influx of soldiers. They had to be accommodated by the town's people, who had already lost some of their houses due to the strengthening of the defences. On 14 June 1645 the Royalist

---

5   A. C. Wood, 'A Note on the Population of Six Nottinghamshire Towns in the 17th Century', *TTS*, 41 (1937). See also Stuart B. Jennings, *'These Uncertaine Tymes': Newark and the Civilian Experience of the Civil Wars, 1640–1660* (Nottingham, Nottinghamshire County Council, 2009),

situation worsened further with the defeat at the Battle of Naseby. In September Prince Rupert was forced to surrender the only remaining first-class Royalist port of Bristol to Sir Thomas Fairfax. There were factions within the Royalist side and one of King Charles' advisers was Sir John Digby, who hated Rupert on a personal basis. Probably on the advice of Digby, Charles decided to dismiss Rupert from his service and send him back to the Continent. Rupert was having none of that, so along with his brother Prince Maurice and 300 troopers rode to Newark, where the King was staying, to confront him. Following a court-martial Rupert was cleared of any wrongdoing in the surrender of Bristol. However, within days it was announced that Sir Richard Willys, who was a supporter of Rupert, was to be replaced as Governor by Lord John Belasyse, who had land at Holme and would thus have local support. Incensed by this news Rupert confronted his uncle, probably in the upper rooms of the Governor's House. During the confrontation swords were reported to have been drawn. The following morning Charles would have witnessed Willys's regiment burning their colours in the Market Place before leaving the town, along with Prince Rupert, Prince Maurice and the 300 troopers, and they made their way to Belvoir Castle. Charles is said to have wept as he watched Rupert leave, knowing he had lost the support of his best cavalry commander. Belasyse took over as Governor and the King left the town as Parliamentarian and Scots forces were converging on it. However, Rupert's men may have left a legacy, as Bristol had had an outbreak of bubonic plague, which may have been brought with them to Newark.

Taking the Outposts

The first task for the attackers was to take Newark's outpost garrisons. On 3 November a force led by Colonel General Sydenham Poyntz and Nottingham's Governor, Colonel John Hutchinson, attacked Shelford Manor, where the garrison was commanded by Sir Philip Stanhope. After Stanhope refused to surrender a frenzied attack was launched during which 160 of the defenders, including women and children, were killed. Dr David Appleby of Nottingham University has recently published his research into possible reasons for the ferocity of the assault.[6] When the Parliamentarian force arrived at Wiverton Hall a week later, some of the Shelford survivors were amongst those in the garrison there. Whether the reputation of what happened at Shelford influenced events or not, the garrison surrendered without a struggle.

---

6   David J. Appleby, 'Fleshing Out a Massacre: the storming of Shelford House and social forgetting in Restoration England', in *Historical Research*, vol. 94, 260 (May, 2020), pp.286–308.

The Siege Begins

As Poyntz's Parliamentarian army of around 9,000 men approached from the south and east a Scots Covenanter army of around 7,000 men approached from the north. The Scots were commanded by Alexander Leslie, Lord Leven. On 26 November 1645 the Scots took Muskham Bridge and the 'island' as the Parliamentarian Army closed in from the south. Soon after establishing the Scots army's positions Alexander Leslie retired to Newcastle, leaving the conduct of the siege in the hands of David Leslie. The besiegers soon established their own earthworks, which can be seen on the siege maps. The Scots headquarters on the 'island' was known as Edinburgh, while Poyntz's headquarters at Hawton became known as London. A bridge of boats was built at Crankley Point where the two arms of the Trent rejoin to maintain communications between the Scots and Parliamentarian Armies. Sconces were built to protect the bridge of boats and also at Sandhills, Tolney Lane, to directly threaten the Queen's Sconce.

Town defences at the time of the final siege. Map by Stuart Fleming (courtesy of NCWC)

The winter of 1645/46 was particularly harsh, but the defenders of Newark were well prepared, knowing a siege was likely. Provisions had been brought in and stockpiled in the town, whereas the besiegers had to forage for their supplies or buy them from neighbouring villages. The Scots were a mainly cavalry force and there are reports of them obtaining forage for their horses from as far away as Derbyshire and South Yorkshire. A line of circumvallation was built around the south of the town, but the initial line had little effect, with reports of Royalists easily able to get beyond them and return. Over the harsh winter the besieged garrison made a number of forays, one of which nearly captured Poyntz and another of which almost re-captured the 'island'. Shortage of money was also going to become a problem, so Governor Bellasyse set up a mint in the castle grounds, which produced the distinctive diamond shaped 'siege pieces'. There were four values, 6 pence, 9 pence, 12 pence (1 shilling) and 30 pence (2 shillings and 6 pence, or half a crown). The values were stamped on one side beneath a crown and the cipher CR for *Carolus Rex*, the Latin for King Charles. On the reverse was stamped OBS Newark and either 1645 or 1646. OBS is short for Latin *Obsessum*, which translates as 'Besieged'. They were made from silver plate, either donated or possibly part of the spoils from the Storm of Leicester, which the Newark garrison participated in.

Newark 'siege pieces'. Left to right: 6 pence, 1 shilling, 9 pence. (Courtesy of NCWC).

Effects of Disease

Disease now came to the fore for the defenders, and over the winter typhus became a problem. With the number of people forced to live with each other, huddled together for warmth and with less regular washing of bodies and clothes, body lice were easily transmitted from person to person. However, from March 1646 on bubonic plague, which may have lain dormant due to the severe winter weather since Prince Rupert's visit, began to spread as the warmer weather arrived.[7] The Borough Minutes[8] record measures taken to try to combat the spread of plague, such as pest houses for shutting up those infected, but as the siege wore on it began to take its toll. The East Stoke Parish Register for 1646 records 178 deaths between March 1646 and March 1647. East Stoke Parish included areas of Newark, including, at that time, the castle. Many would have been infected after the siege ended and people returned to their homes.

The Net Closes

As spring arrived the line of circumvallation was enhanced, bringing it closer to the town and thus more effective. Poyntz also attempted to dam the River Devon to try to prevent the mills on Millgate from producing both flour and gunpowder for the besieged town. This proved unsuccessful. Bellasyse was issued with a summons to surrender, but this was ignored.

Unexpected Developments

Neither besiegers or besieged were aware of developments with the King. Cardinal Mazarin, First Minister of France, had appointed Jean de Montereul as his envoy to the Scots. He was working on negotiations with the Scots to change sides or to reach a separate peace. News reached Oxford that negotiations were advanced enough that the King should travel to Southwell to meet with the Scots Commissioners. On 27 April Charles left Oxford in disguise and, after a winding journey, arrived in Southwell on the morning of 5 May. After resting in what is now the *Saracen's Head*, then the *King's Arms*, he met the Scots Commissioners in the Archbishop's Palace. One of the key demands from the Scots was that Presbyterianism should be established as the religion of the Kingdom of England, something the King was not prepared to concede. He was forced to surrender to the Scots and was taken to Kelham House (now beneath the footprint of Kelham Hall) where he spent the night. The following day he was taken to the Scots encampment of Edinburgh, where he surrendered to David Leslie.

---

7   Stuart B. Jennings, "A Miserable, Stinking, Infected Town': Pestilence, Plague and Death in a Civil War Garrison, Newark, 1640–1649', *Midland History*, 28 (2003), pp.51–70.
8   Nottinghamshire Archives , DC/NW/3/1/1, Borough Minutes.

Surrender

Charles was taken, via the bridge of boats, to Colonel Rossiter's headquarters at Balderton, from where he issued orders to Bellasyse to surrender Newark. It was felt that if the order came from the Parliamentary encampment it would be better received than if it came from the Scots encampment. When Bellasyse and the Mayor received the King's order they were dismayed and wanted to continue. This was when the Mayor is reported to have said 'Trust in God and sally forth', in other words go out and fight. The Latin *Deo Fretus Erumpe* became the town's motto in 1922 and is printed below the crest. However, as Newark was one of the final Royalist garrisons in England and there was no hope of relief it was agreed to surrender the town. On 8 May around 1,800 troops were allowed to march out of the town with colours flying and drums beating, but leaving their arms behind. A Parliamentarian tract, published 5 days later, records the people and arms captured at Newark, including the cannon 'Sweet Lips'.

Tract, *The Kings March with the Scots,* dated 13 May 1646. (courtesy of NCWC)

Aftermath

While the Scots army broke camp and marched to Newcastle with the King as their prisoner, the Parliamentarians entered the town. St Mary Magdalene bore the brunt of the Puritanism of the erstwhile besiegers. Stained glass windows were smashed and the empty niches visible from Church Walk South are evidence of where statues of saints had stood and were destroyed. The font was turned over and broken in two. It was restored in 1660 by a local businessman, Nicholas Ridley. If you look at the font today you can see the bottom part is fourteenth century, made from a different stone and with the figures in fourteenth century clothes. The restored part is made from a different stone and the figures have seventeenth century clothes and hair styles. This destruction is euphemistically known as 'slighting', and the Parliamentarians intended to slight the castle, so that it would not be of use in the future. However, as bubonic plague was now rife the Parliamentarians wanted to get out as soon as they could. Only one barrel of gunpowder was exploded in the castle gatehouse, leaving the arch blackened as it remains to this day. The castle owes its condition as a semi ruin to the fact that it was a convenient source for building materials as it fell further and further into disrepair. The abrupt departure of the Parliamentarians meant that the castle, Queen's Sconce and other buildings and earthworks from the period survived, and their significance was recognised, so that they can still be visited today. Plague spread to the surrounding towns and villages as people returned to their homes and it is estimated that Newark took 150 years to fully recover from the effects of plague.

The Siegeworks Today

Visitors to Newark today can still see remains of the siegeworks. Indeed, the Queen's Sconce is described as the best surviving seventeenth century earthwork in England. Other earthworks still visible are Muskham Sconce, which sits in a field to the left of the current Muskham Bridge as you travel towards South Muskham. At Crankley Point, where the bridge of boats joined the Scots on the 'island' and the Parliamentarians on the southern bank, a Scots redoubt can be found on one side and remnants of Colonel Grey's Sconce on the other. Kelham Lodge Sconce and Sandhills Sconce are also still visible – although an aerial view is probably the best way to see them. Just down the road from the National Civil War Centre Newark Museum is Friary Park, where a bank running along Queen's Road can still be seen. This is the last remnant of the earthworks that once surrounded the town.

The last time the siegeworks were investigated was as part of the Royal Commission on Historical Monuments (England) *Newark-on-Trent, the Civil War Siege Works*[9], published by Her Majesty's Stationery Office in 1964. A new examination of the siegeworks using modern archaeological procedures is long overdue and a group had been formed to start work on this – before Covid intervened. It is very much hoped that the project will be revived at some stage to look at new sites as well as those already known.

Aerial view of Muskham Sconce. Photographer Ian Bracegirdle, (courtesy of NCWC)

9   Royal Commission on Historical Monuments (England) *Newark-on-Trent, the Civil War Siege Works* (London: HMSO, 1964),

Bibliography

Primary Manuscript Sources
Nottinghamshire Archives Office
DC/NW/3/1/1* Newark Borough Council Minutes, 1640–1660
PR/24810, Newark Church Warden Accounts, 1640–1662
PR/27256–27257, Newark Parish Registers, 1640–1660
PR/346, East Stoke Parish Registers

National Civil War Centre – Newark Museum
DC/NW D48.74*, Newark Military Documents, 1642–1648

Nottingham University Manuscripts Department
Me LM 11, Mellish Papers, Twentyman Manuscript,

Secondary Sources
Published
Appleby, D. J. & Hopper, A., eds., A., *Battle-scarred: Mortality, Medical Care and Military Welfare in the British Civil Wars* (Manchester: MUP, 2018)
Brown, C., *A History of Newark-on-Trent*, 2 volumes (Nottingham: Nottinghamshire County Council, 1995; originally published 1904)
Ingham, S., *Discovering the Civil War in Nottinghamshire* (Nottingham: Nottinghamshire County Council, 1992)
Jennings, Stuart B., *These Uncertaine Tymes: Newark and the Civilian Experience of the Civil Wars, 1640–1660* (Nottingham: Nottinghamshire County Council, 2009)
Warner, Tim, *Newark: Civil War and Siegeworks* (Nottingham: Nottinghamshire County Council, 1992)
Wood, Alfred C., *Nottinghamshire in the Civil War* (Wakefield: S. R. Reprint, 1971; originally published 1937)

Journal Articles
Jennings, Stuart B., "'A Miserable, Stinking, Infected Town': Pestilence, Plague and Death in a Civil War Garrison, Newark, 1640–1649', in *Midland History*, 28 (2003), pp.51–70
Jennings, Stuart B., 'The Third and Final Siege of Newark (1645–1646) and the Impact of the Scottish Army upon Nottinghamshire and Adjacent Counties', in *Midland History*, 37:2 (2012), pp.142–162
Jennings, Stuart B., 'The Anatomy of a Civil War Plague in a Rural Parish: East Stoke, Nottinghamshire, 1646', in *Midland History*, 40:2 (2015), pp.201–219

A Small Fort in Devon: How Forty Musketeers Changed History

Nick Arnold

In mid-August 1644 King Charles I took an extraordinary decision. On the eve of a major battle, he chose to risk his lines of communication and weaken the security of an important town in order to rescue a small redoubt defended by 40 musketeers. Appledore Fort, however, was no ordinary redoubt and its garrison was no ordinary garrison. In 2021 the largely forgotten defences of this small fort in North Devon were rediscovered, allowing its historical significance to be appreciated.

Local tradition identifies the site of Appledore Fort with a small earthwork on the summit of Staddon Hill, overlooking the port village of Appledore. White's Devonshire Directory of 1850 describes the earthwork as: '…the site of an ancient fort, supposed to have been built during the civil wars of the seventeenth century.'[1]

Staddon Hill is 'Fort Hill' in both the 1804 first series Ordnance Survey map,[2] and Denham's 1832 map of the Taw-Torridge Estuary.[3] The parish Tithe Map denotes the site as 'Mount Field'.[4] In this context 'Mount' apparently refers to a seventeenth century fortification often constructed of earth such as 'Gloucester Mount' (Lichfield), 'Bury Mount' (Towcester), 'Colston's Mount Fort' (Bristol), 'the Mount' (York) and 'Mount Gould' (Plymouth).

---

1 William White, History, *Gazetteer, and Directory of Devonshire and the City and County of the City of Exeter Comprising a General Survey of the County of Devon and the Diocese of Exeter* (Sheffield: Robert Leader, 1850), p.772.
2 North Devon, Sheet 26 (1:63360), Ordnance Survey, first series 1809,<https://www.visionofbritain.org.uk/maps/series?>, accessed 2 July 2023
3 Denham's Map of Taw-Torridge Estuary 1832 in David Carter, *Illustrated History of Appledore: its place in history* (Appledore: David Carter, 2017), vol. 3, p.94.
4 Tithe Map of Northam 1839, <https://maps.bristol.gov.uk/kyp?edition=devon&mapbse=2017>, accessed May 2021; *Northam Tithe Map Index*, <http://www.genuki.org.uk/big/eng/DEV/Northam/NorthamTithes>, accessed 19May 2021

The earthwork on Staddon Hill is approximately 56 metres above sea level. The ground slopes away on all sides, but more gently towards the west. To the north-east of the site the River Taw leads to Barnstaple, to the east the River Torridge leads to Bideford, and to the north the combined estuary of the two rivers joins the sea. The site has commanding views of both rivers and the estuary.

Three-dimensional Lidar view of Staddon Hill, showing the position of Appledore Fort in relation to the Taw-Torridge estuary, the two rivers and the historic settlement of Appledore village. (1m DSM data, Lidar Map rendering provided by houseprices.io lab)

View from Appledore Fort looking north-east and showing the rivers to Barnstaple and Bideford. (Author's photo)

This wide panoramic of the two rivers is only possible from the summit of Staddon Hill and therefore the earthwork is the only possible location for the fort mentioned by The Earl of Clarendon, in his history of the Civil War: '...the fort at Appledore, which commanded the river to Barnstaple and Biddeford being delivered to Colonel Digby... [August 1643]'.[5] There are several contemporary references to Appledore Fort's control of the riverine access to Barnstaple but Clarendon's description is of particular interest because he probably saw the Fort. In 1645 he was an adviser to Prince Charles (later Charles II) and he doubtless accompanied the Prince on a visit to Appledore on 10 July.[6]

Despite their identification as a Civil War fort, the earthworks are so damaged and altered that it is hard for the modern visitor to make sense of them. The most obvious feature on the site is a large shed, built in 1995.The shed stands on a low rise and to the south is an elongated dip and a 0.10 metre rise 18 metres long and between 4.5 metres and 10.5 metres wide. A later field bank bounds the west of the site. On the eastern side of the site is an irregular mound 2.3 metres high and 9 metres in diameter.

View of Fort site from the east showing the mound (with the modern shed behind it). The earthwork on the right is the eastern end of the northern rampart. Immediately in front of it are the foundations of the later stone building. (Author's photo)

5   Earl of Clarendon, *The History of the Rebellion and Civil War in England begun in the year 1641* (Oxford: Clarendon Press, 1888), vol. 3, p.168.
6   Richard W. Cotton, *Barnstaple and Northern Part of Devon during the Great Civil War 1642–1646*(London: Unwin Brothers, 1889), p.388, n.2.

Immediately to the north of the mound are the foundations of a rough stone building measuring 5.5 metres east–west and 7.5 metres north-south. The building is cut into the eastern end of what must be an earlier east–west bank exposing its rubble core. This earlier east–west bank is up to 7.5 metres wide, 1.4 metres high and approximately 25 metres long. On the northern side of the bank, and extending along much of its length, is a slight dip approximately 5 metres wide and up to 0.10 metres deep.[7] Immediately to the north of the building and connected to the east–west bank is a projecting flattened rise. Lidar and magnetometry images show that the dip deviates to the north to allow for the flattened projecting feature.

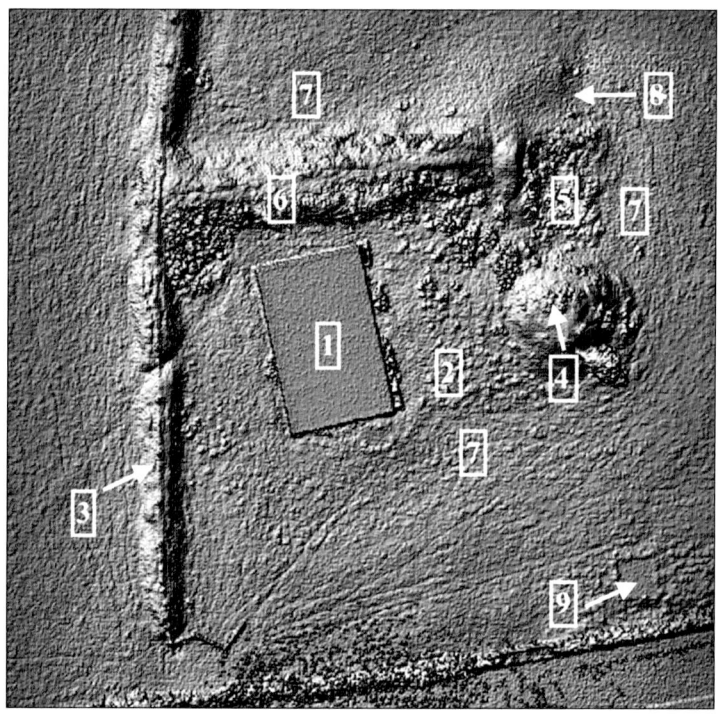

DSM Lidar view of Fort site showing main features. (1) Modern shed; (2) Flattened southern rampart; Later western field bank; (4) Mound covering site of eastern rampart; (5) Site of later stone building; (6) Northern rampart; (7) In-filled ditch; (8) Flattened demi-bastion; (9) Later well (South West Surveys Ltd.)

---

7   T. H. Gent, *Archaeological Observations at Staddon Hill, Appledore* (Exeter: Exeter Archaeology, 1995), p.1; Devon and Dartmoor Historic Environment Record MDV11870 – Civil War Fort on Staddon Hill, Northam, <http://wwww.heritagegateway.org.uk/gateway/Results-Single.aspx?uid=MDV11870&resourceID=104>, accessed 19 May 2021

Any investigation of the Fort's defences faced the daunting challenge of interpreting the site. For example, the first researcher to study the site, Richard W. Cotton, who visited the site at some time before 1889, mistakenly described the defences as: '...evidently quadrangular, with bastions at the angles, one of which with traces of a revetment is tolerably well preserved.'[8] This sounds like a sconce fort typified by the Queen's Sconce in Newark-on-Trent. However, the purported corner bastions are found in no aerial photograph, Lidar or magnetometry image. The 'well preserved' bastion must be the projecting flattened feature because the 'traces of revetment' Cotton noted are still visible in the eastern end of the northern bank.

Eastern end of the northern rampart showing its exposed rubble core. At its base are the remains of a rough stone revetment. This is the feature that Cotton interpreted as 'traces of a revetment'. (Author's photo)

---

8   Cotton, *Barnstaple*, p.297.

More recent analysis of Lidar images and aerial photographs demonstrate that Appledore Fort was in fact a small four-sided redoubt with a single demi-bastion at its north-eastern corner. A demi-bastion is a half-bastion with a single flank and face designed to protect the main rampart. This interpretation of the site is supported by data from a magnetometry survey in May 2021,[9] and a more detailed Lidar survey of the site in November 2021.

It is now clear that the northern bank and dip is the northern rampart and ditch. The projecting feature at the eastern end of the northern rampart is the flattened demi-bastion. The mound and the later stone building foundations cover the eastern rampart, and the western field bank partly covers any remains of the western rampart. The rise on which the shed stands is the flattened southern rampart. On the eastern, southern, and possibly the western sides of the fort, the ditch survives as a largely in-filled feature and there are traces of a possible counterscarp bank on the northern, eastern and southern sides.

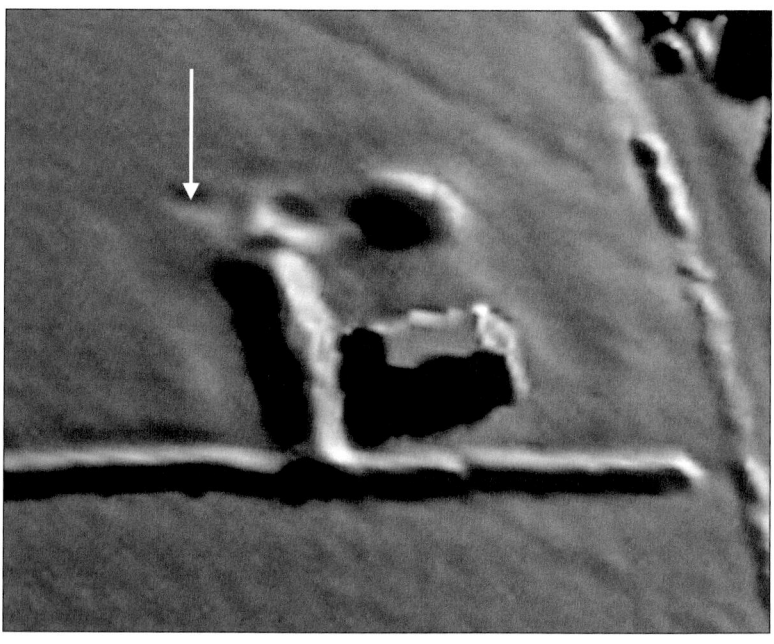

Three-dimensional Lidar view of the Appledore Fort site. The largely in-filled ditch is just visible on three sides. The flattened demi-bastion is arrowed. (1m DSM data, Lidar Map rendering provided by houseprices.io lab)

9 Mark Edwards, *An Archaeological Magnetometer Survey, Land at Staddon Hill, Appledore Centred on NGR: 246125, 130677 Report: 2104APP-R-1* (Bideford: Substrata Ltd., 2021).

A SMALL FORT IN DEVON

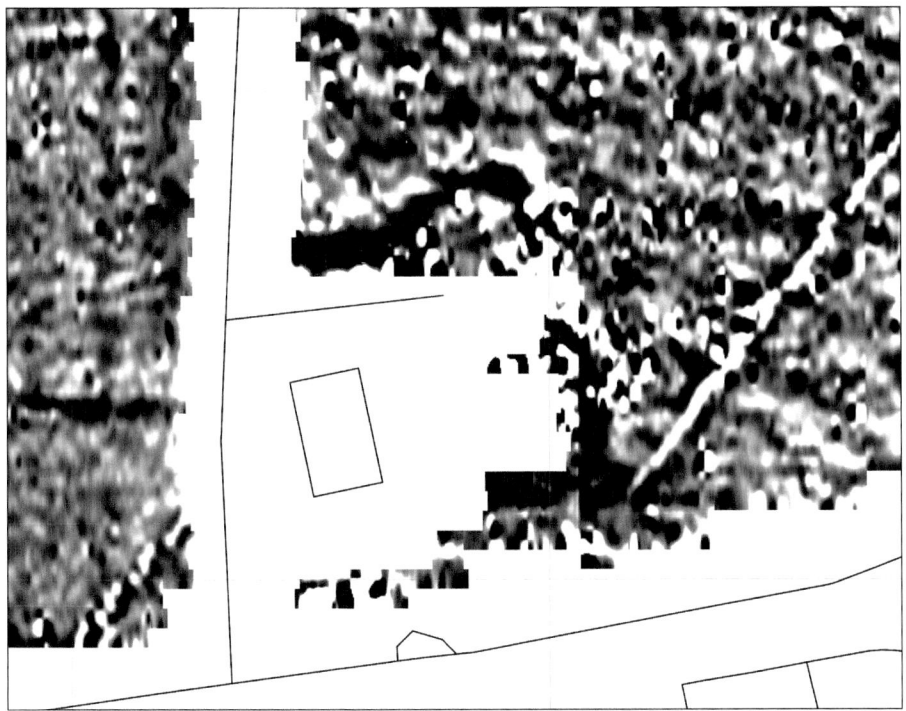

Processed magnetometer image of the Fort site. The dark marks show the position of the ditches. The line of the northern ditch deviates at its eastern end to allow for the demi-bastion. (Substrata Ltd. 2021)

Contemporary military manuals describe four-sided redoubts comprising an earthen bank and ditch. For example, in his influential *Animadversions of Warre*, Robert Ward terms this fieldwork a 'Quadrangle Redout'.[10] Although quadrangle redoubts were simple four-sided structures, during the Civil War they were more varied.[11] Ward himself describes a type of quadrangle redoubt with 'angles' (demi-bastions) described as a 'Flankered Redout: 'This kinde of Redout is the strongest, and can best defend itselfe, in regard every side hath an Angle to Flanke it...'[12]

---

10 Robert Ward, *Animadversions of Warre or, a militarie magazine of the truest rules and ablest instructions for the managing of warre* (London: John Dawson, 1639), p.87.
11 Peter Harrington, *English Civil War Fortifications 1642–1651* (Oxford: Osprey, 2003), pp.10, 24–25, 33–34.
12 Ward, *Animadversions*, p.105.

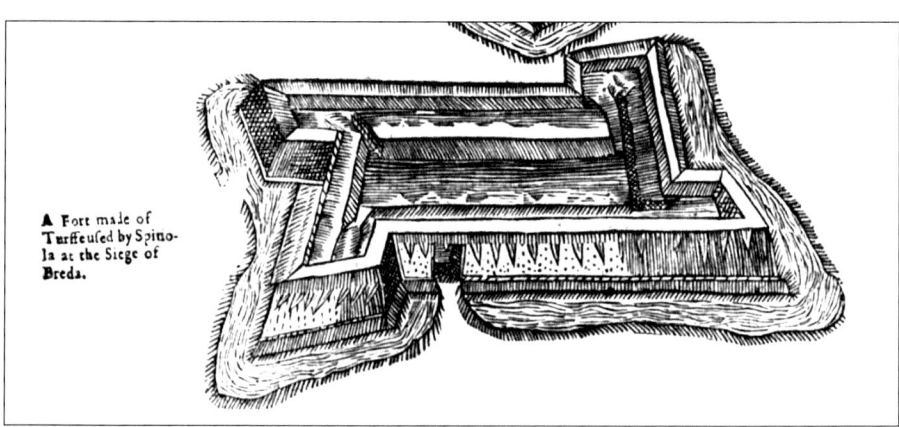

'Flankered' quadrangle redoubts illustrated in Robert Ward's Animadversions of Warre. (Public Domain)

It is clear from Lidar images that the projecting feature at Appledore Fort is in the same position, shape and size relative to the fort as one of the 'angles' illustrated by Ward. The projecting feature also matches a demi-bastion of a Civil War fort built by the Scots during the siege of Newark.[13] A contemporary plan describes this fieldwork as a 'flanked redout of the Scots by the Red Lodge'.[14] Appledore Fort was therefore a redoubt of the same type, albeit with only one demi-bastion instead of four.

Northern rampart of Appledore Fort viewed from the north-east. The flattened demi-bastion is the raised area in the foreground. (Author's photo)

Although no records describe Appledore Fort, details of its likely appearance can be inferred from military manuals and other Civil War fieldworks. Ward recommended palisading a redoubt commanding an important passage[15] and Appledore Fort probably had a palisade on top of its ramparts. The Fort undoubtedly required cannon and they would have been mounted behind the ramparts on wooden platforms.[16] In accordance with usual practice, nearby field boundaries would have been removed to create a clear field of fire.[17] Magnetometry indicates multiple former field boundaries to the west of the Fort.[18]

13 One-metre Lidar image of demi-bastion at Grid reference SK7873054444 viewable at <https://houseprices.io/lab/lidar/map?ref=SK79145449>, accessed 8 June 2023
14 Civil War redoubt 680 m north west of Dairy Farm 10168048: Official list entry, Historic England, < https://historicengland.org.uk/listing/the-list/list-entry/1016048?section=official-list-entry>, accessed 8 June 2023
15 Ward, *Animadversions*, p.106.
16 Harrington, *Fortifications*, p.38.
17 Harrington, *Fortifications*, p.18.
18 Edwards, *Magnetometer Survey*, pp.3, 5.

Like other forts, Appledore Fort possibly contained wooden buildings for storage and accommodation.[19] The interior was apparently roughly cobbled. In 1995 T. H. Gent (Exeter Archaeology) exposed part of a cobbled surface and its orientation matched the Fort's defences rather than the later stone building.

To the south of the fort site a rough cobbled lane led to the road to Appledore village. The lane was aligned with a feature that Gent identified as a possible entrance to the Fort through the 'low linear east–west bank' of the southern rampart.[20] Although the lane is now lost under modern housing, it is described as being about 135 metres long and 1.7 metres wide.[21] Since the lane apparently pre-dates the later flattening of the southern rampart, it may have been constructed as an access lane to the Fort. While a cobbled interior and access lane are unusual in a Civil War fieldwork, the access is quite steep and a cobbled lane would have made it easier to transport cannon or heavy carts to the Fort.

Appledore Fort site from the south. The flattened southern rampart is the raised area to the left of the mound. The evening sun shines on the largely in-filled southern ditch. (Author's photo)

Appledore Fort was probably constructed early in 1643. By January 1643 there were Parliamentary garrisons in Bideford and Barnstaple, and Barnstaple was being fortified.[22] In his history of Bideford published in 1792, John Watkins wrote:

---

19 Harrington, *Fortifications*, p.22.
20 Gent, *Archaeological Observations*, p.1.
21 Witness Statement: Mrs Jenny Arnold in Nick Arnold, *Historical and Archaeological Report: Appledore Fort, Staddon Hill, Appledore, Devon* (unpublished, 2021), p.14.
22 Cotton, *Barnstaple*, p.111.

> Two forts were erected in Bideford, one on the highest part of each side of the river [Torridge] so as to command completely both that and the whole town. The most considerable of these forts was provided with eight cannon, and being erected by the Parliament's forces under the command of Major-General James Chudleigh, was called after his name. There is also a small fort erected at Appledore, which effectually commanded the entrance of both the rivers [Torridge and Taw] to Bideford and Barnstaple.[23]

(The second Bideford fort was West-the-Water Fort.) Watkins's source is unknown but he may have had access to oral tradition or lost archival sources in Bideford. His account is supported by considerable circumstantial evidence.

Unlike some other Civil War commanders, James Chudleigh recognised the value of fortifications. During a local truce from 28 February to 22 April 1643 his men built fortifications to protect the approaches to Okehampton.[24] Chudleigh later changed sides and was killed at the siege of Dartmouth in October 1643.[25]

Morphological similarities between Chudleigh and Appledore forts suggest that the same person planned them. Today Chudleigh Fort has been replaced by a Victorian belvedere, which largely preserves its outline and the Bideford Tithe Map confirms that the Fort was a quadrangle redoubt of similar shape to Appledore Fort.[26] Each fort had two approximate right angles, one obtuse angle and one acute angle, although Chudleigh Fort apparently lacked a demi-bastion. As Watkins claimed, Chudleigh Fort was slightly larger than Appledore Fort.

West-the-Water Fort was destroyed around 1848,[27] when its earthworks were robbed of stones to build a folly.[28] In 1953 Major William Ascott, presumably relying on a local tradition, located the Fort in Bull's Close Field overlooking the River Torridge from the west.[29] Modern housing covers the site but according to Ascott, the Fort was 'similar to Chudleigh Fort' and so by extension it must have

---

23   John Watkins, *A History of Bideford in the County of Devon*, (Bideford: Edward Gaskell Publishers, 1993), p.46.
24   Cotton, *Barnstaple*, pp.147 – 148.
25   *Dictionary of National Biography*, Chudleigh, James 1617–1643, <https://doi.org/10.1093/ref:odnb/5382>
26   Field707, Tithe Map of Bideford 1841, <https://maps.bristol.gov.uk/kyp?edition–devon&mapbse–2017>, accessed 19 May 2021
27   Historic England, The Folly including boundary walls on north and south sides 1200932: Official list entry, <https://historicengland.org.uk/listing/the-list/list-entry/1200932?section=official-list-entry>, accessed 16 June 2023
28   Major W. Ascott, *Random Notes of Old Bideford and District* (Bideford: Bideford Gazette,1953), p.15.
29   Field 720, Tithe Map of Bideford 1841, <https://maps.bristol.gov.uk/kyp?edition=devon&mapbse=2017>, accessed 19 May 2021 *Bideford Tithe Apportionments*

been similar to Appledore Fort.[30] A drawing of Bideford by G. B. Campion and published as an engraving in 1831 shows a small and partly overgrown four-sided enclosure in the identified location of West-the-Water Fort. The distinctive shape of this feature is indeed similar to Chudleigh Fort and Appledore Fort.[31]

Detail from *Bideford, Devon,* drawn by G. B. Campion and engraved by James Bingley. The four-sided enclosure arrowed matches the description and reported location of West-the-Water Fort. (Author's photo)

The locations of Chudleigh Fort and the identified site of West-the-Water Fort would have been visible to Watkins in the 1790s and they are consistent with his description of forts designed to command the river and Bideford town. Beside the need to defend against enemy shipping, the Bideford forts had to protect the

(transcript), <https://www.devon.gov.uk/historicenvironment/tithe-map/bideford/>, accessed 19 May 2021
30 Ascott, *Random Notes,* p.15.
31 *Bideford, Devon,* drawn by G. B. Campion, engraved by James Bingley (London: Jennings and Chaplin, 1831), (property of N. Arnold), image available online at: <https://www.gettyimages.co.uk/detail/news-photo/bideford-devon-circa-1790-engraved-by-james-bingley-after-a-news-photo/110263914>, accessed 2 July 2023

town from the east. From this direction the town was accessed across the narrow bridge, but at low tide the town was vulnerable to attack across the riverbed. As Defoe noted in the 1720s: 'the carts and waggons go over the sand with great ease and safety;'[32]

Chudleigh Fort was sited on a hill slope covering the River Torridge and Bideford Bridge. West-the-Water Fort was 700 metres across the river from Chudleigh Fort. This was also a hill slope with steep slopes to the east and north and a gentler slope to the south. From here the cannon of West-the-Water Fort could cover the River Torridge, Bideford Bridge and southern Bideford. The two forts would have been inter-visible and able to protect each other with flanking fire.

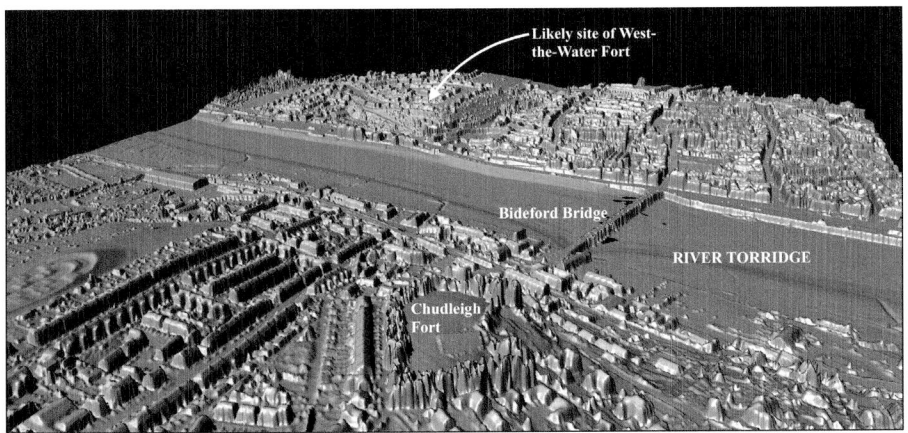

Three-dimensional Lidar view of Bideford showing Chudleigh Fort (visible as a raised platform) and the likely site of West-the-Water Fort in relation to Bideford Bridge and the River Torridge. (1m DSM data, Lidar Map rendering provided by houseprices.io lab)

Despite being 4km north of Bideford, Appledore Fort was part of this defensive system because, as Watkins noted, it controlled the estuarine access to Bideford and Barnstaple. The strong tides and sandbanks of the estuary required ships to proceed cautiously and any passing sailing ship would have been highly vulnerable to cannon fire from the Fort. Indeed Appledore Fort's demi-bastion extended its

---

32   Daniel Defoe, *A tour thro' the whole island of Great Britain, divided into circuits or journies, Letter IV Containing a description of the north shore of the counties of Cornwall, and Devon, and some parts of Somersetshire, Wiltshire, Dorsetshire, Gloucestershire, Buckinghamshire and Berkshire* (London: J. M. Dent and Co., 1927), <https://www.visionofbritain.org.uk/travellers/Defoe/15>

eastern rampart, enabling more guns to fire on the River Torridge. In 1639 ferries had been established between Appledore and Instow (across the River Torridge) and between Appledore and Braunton (across the combined Torridge and Taw estuaries).[33] Appledore Fort commanded both ferry crossings.

The positions of the three forts suggest they formed a carefully planned defensive system to protect Bideford from riverine attack and to control river crossing points. This conforms to advice in contemporary military manuals. Both Ward,[34] and his fellow military writer, Henry Hexham,[35] recommended the use of small quadrangle forts sited on high ground to protect waterways and river crossings. The fact that the forts were smaller than Ward recommended,[36] may have been due to a shortage of garrison troops.

The focus on the riverine defence reflected Bideford's importance as a port and made military sense in the opening months of 1643. At this time, Hopton's Royalist army was penned in Cornwall and the greatest threat to the North Devon ports came from privateers based in the Cornish ports that might have been tempted to enter the estuary and attack shipping.[37]

The fact that the Bideford forts were also positioned to defend the town against land attack from the south or east proved a wise precaution because the Royalists were hoping to capture the North Devon ports in 1643. During the Civil War both sides sought to control ports because they provided tax revenues and enabled food, war materials and reinforcements to be supplied by sea.[38]

On 8 February 1643 the Royalist newspaper *Mercurius Aulicus* incorrectly claimed that the Royalists had taken Bideford and their leader Sir Bevil Grenville: 'will quickly master Barnstaple, being already master of the Haven there and consequently of the mouth of the Severn.'[39] The 'Haven' at 'the mouth of the Severn' was actually the Taw and Torridge estuary at Appledore. It is unclear whether the writer knew of Appledore Fort, but his prescient comment that taking Appledore would enable the Royalists to control Barnstaple indicates that he was aware of Appledore's strategic position.

33 William Douglas Hamilton, *Calendar of State Papers, Domestic Series of the Reign of Charles I, Preserved in the State Papers Department of Her Majesty's Public Record Office 1639 – 40* (London: Longman and Co., 1877), vol. 15, pp.66–116, <http://www.british-history.ac.uk/cal-state-papers/domestic/chas1/1639-40/>, accessed 19 May 2021
34 Ward, *Animadversions*, p.87.
35 Henry Hexham, *The Principles of the Art Military, as practised in the warres of the United Netherlands, Part 2* (Delft: Jan Pieters Walpote, 1638), p.23.
36 Ward, *Animadversions*, p.58.
37 John Barratt, *Civil War in the South-West: 1642–1646* (Barnsley: Pen and Sword Books Ltd, 2005), p.30.
38 John Barratt, *Sieges of the English Civil War* (Barnsley: Pen and Sword Books, 2008), p.86.
39 Cotton, *Barnstaple*, p.109.

In April 1643 the Royalists sent soldiers disguised as civilians to capture Bideford. Unfortunately one man got drunk and revealed the plan.[40] The Royalists eventually succeeded in taking the ports after Colonel John Digby routed the Bideford and Barnstaple garrisons in a skirmish in August. The skirmish took place at Torrington, a small market town on the River Torridge 8.5km south-east of Bideford.[41]

According to Clarendon, instead of besieging Bideford or Barnstaple, Digby headed directly for Appledore.[42] Since no source mentions a siege, it appears that Appledore Fort surrendered promptly on generous terms around 21 August. Like the author of the *Mercurius Aulicus* report, Digby clearly recognised Appledore's strategic position and used the Fort to blockade Bideford and Barnstaple. Digby's force had been detached from Sir John Berkeley's army, which was then besieging Exeter, and Digby's tactics may have been informed by Berkeley's use of artillery to block the riverine access to Exeter and prevent the Parliamentary navy from relieving the town.[43]

Colonel John Digby, who captured Appledore Fort in August 1643. ('Colonel Digby', Inkerman Rogers, page 16., *A Concise History of Bideford* (Bideford: Bideford Gazette Printing Service, 1938))

40 Cotton, *Barnstaple*, p.144.
41 Cotton, *Barnstaple*, p.206.
42 Clarendon, *History of the Rebellion*, pp.168–169.
43 Clarendon, *History of the Rebellion*, pp.165–166.

Prince Maurice, the Royalist commander in the South-West, offered the Mayor of Barnstaple terms for surrender on 27 August.[44] The surrender of Appledore and Bideford was certified at Oxford on 2 September,[45] and Barnstaple surrendered on the same day.[46]

Parliamentary journalists blamed the loss of all three North Devon ports on treachery and, in the cases of Bideford and Barnstaple, on treacherous local mayors.[47] In reality continued resistance was hopeless. The Barnstaple and Bideford garrisons must have been demoralised and they had lost men and equipment at Torrington. By using Appledore Fort's strategic control of the river, Digby prevented the garrisons from being resupplied by sea and ensured their rapid surrender.

The Barnstaple Parliamentarians were unwilling to countenance Royalist demands for support and funding. In February 1644, there seems to have been a plot to take over the town.[48] Prince Maurice dispatched troops to Barnstaple and he then apparently installed garrisons at Barnstaple and Bideford.[49] Both ports certainly had Royalist garrisons by the end of June 1644. At the same time the Prince also sent 40 Cornish troops to garrison Appledore Fort. In the words of King Charles I's Secretary for War Sir Edward Walker, the men were sent to Appledore 'in order to make the river useless to that town [Barnstaple].'[50] The Royalist national leadership were now aware of Appledore Fort's strategic importance.

Although *Mercurius Aulicus* described the 40 Cornish soldiers as 'musketeers' they presumably also included artillerymen, capable of firing the fort's cannon.[51] Judging by their performance in 1644, these men were selected for their reliability, rather than being volunteers seeking a comfortable alternative to service in the field.[52]

Life at Appledore Fort was far from comfortable. Harrington suggests that the living accommodation may not have been inside the fort. In this case some of the garrison may have camped adjacent to the defences or lodged in Appledore

---

44 Cotton, *Barnstaple*, pp.212–214.
45 Cotton, *Barnstaple*, p.217, n.1.
46 Cotton, *Barnstaple*, p.216.
47 Cotton, *Barnstaple*, pp.219–221.
48 Cotton, *Barnstaple*, p.243.
49 Cotton, *Barnstaple*, pp.235–240.
50 Sir Edward Walker, *Historical Discourses upon Several Occasions* (London: Sam. Keble, 1705), p.65.
51 P. Thomas (ed.), *The English Revolution III: Oxford Royalist* (London: Cornmarket Press 1971), p.228.
52 Barratt, *Sieges*, p.29.

village and worked in shifts to guard the fort.[53] Staddon Hill is an exposed place, and without adequate shelter, life for the men guarding the fort would have been uncomfortable, especially in winter. The Cornishmen spent two winters there.

The harsh living conditions at the Fort were aggravated by a shortage of water and inadequate rations for the garrison. Because there was no well at the Fort, the garrison doubtless relied on stored rainwater. (There is now a well south-east of the Fort site but it is outside the defences. Judging by its internal form and brickwork, it dates from the eighteenth century.)

Mercurius Aulicus blamed the food shortage on a Royalist officer: 'a Colonel who is no Cornish man being entrusted to see it victualled but it seemed had neglected it.'[54] The non-Cornish officer was most likely the Colonel in charge of the Bideford garrison. Presumably this officer felt that his own men had first call on food supplies.

Meanwhile the garrison of Appledore Fort probably supplemented their meagre diet with shellfish since numerous mussel and oyster shells are eroding from the mound at the fort site. Given that the Fort was garrisoned from 1643 to 1646 it is quite likely that the site contains sub-surface deposits dating from this occupation. Gent reported pottery finds and a clay pipe stem that may be seventeenth or eighteenth century. Similar finds are eroding from the mound.[55]

In late June 1644 Prince Maurice weakened the garrison by detaching cavalry to escort the Queen to Exeter and the Parliamentarians seized the opportunity to recapture their town.[56] On 1 July the Parliamentarians repulsed Colonel Digby's attempt to recapture the town,[57] and their leaders appealed for help from the Earl of Essex, who was then leading a Parliamentary army into Devon.[58] On 3 July, Essex sent Lord Robartes to secure the town. Robartes' force reached Barnstaple the next day.

On 12 July, for the benefit of its Royalist readers, *Mercurius Aulicus* reacted to the news from Barnstaple with a show of insouciance, claiming that the revolt was futile:

---

53 Peter Harrington (2021), 'New English Civil War fort and siege site found in Devon, England', email (17 Aug. 2021).
54 Thomas (ed.), *The English Revolution III*, p.228.
55 Gent, *Archaeological Observations*, pp.1–2.
56 Cotton, *Barnstaple*, p.254.
57 Cotton, *Barnstaple*, pp.261–271.
58 Barratt, *Civil War*, p.126.

'For its next neighbour *Biddeford* is possessed by a very good Garrison for his Majestie, and being very strongly fortified; besides *Northam* Fort, which fully commands the River below *Barnstaple*.'[59] 'Northam Fort' was, of course, Appledore Fort and the confidence of the Royalist press was not misplaced. As *Mercurius Aulicus* implied, Appledore Fort was well-sited to blockade Barnstaple's riverine access. The port of Barnstaple was now at a standstill and the garrison was short of arms, gunpowder and match. Colonel John Luttrell had requested these supplies from South Wales on 25 June but had not received them.[60] On 12 July Luttrell enquired if the supplies had been sent.[61]

Although Essex and Robartes expected Barnstaple to supply men for their campaign in the West Country, this was impossible owing to the garrison's shortage of arms and ammunition. In fact, far from receiving reinforcements, Robartes was forced to leave three companies of his own men to protect the town when he left Barnstaple in mid-July.[62] The Barnstaple leadership attempted to raise more men, but without supplies they were still powerless to help Robartes when he requested reinforcements at the end of the month.[63]

In order to enable the re-supply of Barnstaple it was now imperative that Appledore Fort was re-taken and Colonel Luttrell took command of an expedition to accomplish this task. According to *Mercurius Aulicus* Luttrell led 'all the men of Barnstaple...'[64] While this was an obvious exaggeration, Luttrell presumably took his own regiment of 374 men,[65] and quite possibly some of the three companies left by Lord Robartes.

Cotton plausibly suggests that Luttrell's force came by river to surprise the Fort.[66] *Mercurius Aulicus* reported that: 'The Fort had sooner been relieved but the Rebels had so closely begirt it that none of His Majesties forces received the least notice of its being so distressed'.[67] By using the River Taw, Luttell's force would have avoided crossing the River Torridge on Bideford Bridge under the guns of the Royalist forts, and this explains why Bideford did not know (at least initially) that Appledore Fort was under siege. Cotton places the attack towards the end of July,

---

59 Thomas (ed.), *The English Revolution III*, p.171. Appledore Fort commanded the river to Barnstaple and it is the only known English Civil War fort in Northam Parish.
60 Cotton, *Barnstaple*, pp.255–257.
61 Cotton, *Barnstaple*, pp.277–278.
62 Cotton, *Barnstaple*, pp.279–280.
63 Cotton, *Barnstaple*, pp.293–294.
64 Thomas (ed.), *The English Revolution III*, p.228.
65 Cotton, *Barnstaple*, p.299.
66 Cotton, *Barnstaple*, p.299.
67 Thomas (ed.), *The English Revolution III*, p.228.

but a surprise dawn attack would have been more practicable a week or so later. As a local landowner, Luttrell would have been familiar with the river and its tides,[68] and high tide was close to dawn around 7 August.[69]

As the siege began the 40 musketeers found themselves in a hopeless position. They were greatly outnumbered and surely demoralised by their Colonel's neglect. According to *Mercurius Aulicus* they were 'much straitened both for bread and fresh water.'[70] In addition the Fort's defences were inadequate. Small redoubts were intended to control communications and annoy the enemy, but not to withstand sieges when isolated from supporting forces. Appledore Fort had rapidly surrendered in 1643 and Luttrell surely expected a similar outcome this time. Yet remarkably, according to *Mercurius Aulicus,* the 40 musketeers resolved to hold the fort '…until the last minute'.[71]

There is no evidence of any siegeworks and quite probably none were necessary. To the north and east the slope of Staddon Hill provided ample cover to within 120 metres of the Fort. There was a sunken lane 100 metres to the west and a large curvilinear bank 150 metres to the south. These features would have enabled the besiegers to create a tight cordon around the Fort without the need for siegeworks.

Three-dimensional Lidar view of the Appledore Fort site from the south. The white line shows the possible siege cordon around the Fort. (1m DSM data, Lidar Map rendering provided by houseprices.io lab)

68 Cotton, *Barnstaple*, p.255, n.1.
69 UK Hydrographic Office Admiralty Easytide, Tidal predictions, Appledore August 1644, (all dates adjusted to Julian calendar 1644).
70 Thomas (ed.), *The English Revolution III*, p.228.
71 Thomas (ed.), *The English Revolution III*, p.228.

The siege appears to have been more than a passive blockade. A seventeenth century musket ball reportedly found in the garden to the west of Staddon (house) may have been fired from the fort.[72] According to *Mercurius Aulicus* the 'valiant Cornish' killed more than 120 besiegers,[73] and Walker reported 100 casualties.[74] Civil War casualty claims are always suspect but the besiegers certainly suffered some casualties because on 10 August a soldier was buried at Northam Church, with a second buried on 12 August.[75] These men perhaps died of wounds or were important enough to be buried in a churchyard. Other casualties were likely interred south of the curving bank, where the Parliamentarians must have been sheltering. The parish tithe map denotes this field (1079) as 'Burying Ground'.[76] The reportedly large number of Parliamentary casualties may have resulted from an unsuccessful attempt to storm the Fort. Such an attempt is plausible given the Parliamentarians' numerical superiority and reported lack of powder.

During the siege the weather was often wet, windy and chilly,[77] and the thirsty garrison would have been grateful for the rainwater to replenish their supplies. Meanwhile, regardless of any failed assault, the Parliamentarians would have remained confident of starving the garrison into surrender.

Around mid-August news of the siege reached the King's army in Cornwall. The Royalist leadership were concerned because a Parliamentary force led by Sir John Middleton and consisting of 2,000 horse and dragoons had reached Somerset. According to Walker, Middleton had been dispatched '...both to hinder our Provisions out of *Somersetshire*, and to endeavour to join with *Essex*.'[78]

Although Middleton's force lacked the numbers to fight their way through to Essex and Sir Francis Dodington's Royalist force was effectively blocking their advance in Somerset,[79] this situation could change if Appledore Fort were to surrender, allowing Barnstaple to be resupplied by sea. The Barnstaple garrison numbered around 900 men. Providing the garrison were adequately armed and

---

72   A. Boyle (2021), 'Can you help me – history of the fort on Staddon Hill'. Email (14 April 2021).
73   Thomas (ed.), *The English Revolution III*, p.228.
74   Walker, *Historical Discourses*, p.65.
75   'Northam Burials 1538–1649', <http://www.genuki.org.uk/big/eng/DEV/Northam/NorthamBurials1538–1649>, accessed 19 May 2021
76   Tithe Map of Northam 1839, <https://maps.bristol.gov.uk/kyp?edition=devon&mapbse=2017>, accessed 19 May 2021; *Northam Tithe Map Index*,<http://www.genuki.org.uk/big/eng/DEV/Northam/NorthamTithes>, accessed 19 May 2021
77   Appledore had the same weather as Cornwall; Barratt, *Civil War*, p.151, p.152.
78   Walker, *Historical Discourses*, p.64.
79   Cotton, *Barnstaple*, p.328.

supplied, they could join with Middleton's force and pose a more serious threat to the Royalist lines of communication.[80]

According to Walker, the King directed Sir John Berkeley, now serving as Governor of Exeter, to relieve Appledore Fort. On 17 August Berkeley ordered his deputy, Colonel Sir Allen Apsley, to undertake this mission with a detachment of the Exeter garrison.[81] Apsley was the brother of the Civil War diarist Lucy Hutchinson, and although Lucy Hutchinson and her husband were Parliamentarians, Apsley and his brother were staunch Royalists.[82]

A letter Berkeley wrote to Colonel Edward Seymour in the Royalist garrison of Dartmouth confirms Walker's account: '…having sent to the relief of Appledore, by His Majesty's command 500 under Colonel Apsley…'[83] Apsley's force probably included elements from his foot and horse regiments, both of which served under him at Exeter in 1644.[84] The dispatch of Apsley's force weakened the Exeter garrison. In his letter to Seymour, Berkeley explained that he was unable to send men to Seymour because Prince Maurice and now Apsley had depleted the Exeter garrison.

A letter by Colonel Sir Hugh Pollard, the commander at Dartmouth, reveals that Apsley picked up reinforcements en-route to Appledore: 'a many of Dodington's horse at Chimleigh [Chumleigh], to the relief of the fort at Appledore, which is strictly besieged by those of Barnstaple.'[85] The diversion of Dodington's cavalry from fending off Middleton again shows the importance the Royalist leadership attached to relieving Appledore Fort. Clearly, the temporary weakening of the Exeter garrison and Dodington's force were considered acceptable risks to ensure Royalist control of Appledore Fort and the continued blockade of Barnstaple.

On 20 August, Apsley's force approached Appledore, but there was to be no battle. The Parliamentarians retreated, most likely to boats on the river as there was no land route to escape by. In their rapid retreat they almost certainly abandoned much of their equipment and their limited supplies of powder.

The Parliamentarian newssheet *Mercurius Civicus* somewhat opaquely blamed the failure of the siege on an unspecified 'late accident'.[86] Meanwhile *Mercurius*

---

80 Barratt, *Civil War*, pp.146–147.
81 Walker, *Historical Discourses*, p.65.
82 *Dictionary of National Biography*, Apsley, Sir Allen 1616–1683, <https://doi.org/10.1093/ref:odnb/600>, accessed 19 May 2021 In 1649 Colonel John Hutchinson was one of the regicides. In 1649 Apsley was able to save him from execution.
83 Lady Rosalind Northcote, *Devon Its Moorland, Streams and Coasts* (London: Chatto and Windus, 1908), p.211.
84 Colonel Sir Allen Apsley: British Civil War Project regimental Wiki <http://wiki.bcw-project.org/start>, accessed 19 May 2021
85 Northcote, *Devon*, p.211.
86 Cotton, *Barnstaple*, p.300.

Aulicus gleefully reported that, 'the well-beaten rebels fled home to Barnstaple so piteously wearied out that they were glad so fair an occasion made them quit their siege.'[87] Wearied or not, the Parliamentarians were surely demoralised by the wretched weather and their failure to take the fort. In addition, if they had stayed, they risked being trapped with limited ammunition and a hostile fort at their backs.

Apsley's rapid advance through hostile territory to surprise a besieging force stands comparison with Sir Henry Gage's relief of Basing House the following month.[88] For the Parliamentarians it was a disaster. Their Admiral, the Earl of Warwick, had just warned the Committee of Both Kingdoms that Barnstaple was 'in sore straits by want of ammunition'.[89] Although the Royalist leadership in Cornwall remained concerned about the threat from Middleton,[90] any threat from Barnstaple had diminished because there was now little chance of supplies reaching the town.

The only alternative to taking supplies past Appledore Fort was to import them via the port of Ilfracombe on the north coast of Devon. However this was not attempted, most likely because the Barnstaple to Ilfracombe road was unsuitable for carts and heavy loads,[91] and supplies transported that way were in danger of being intercepted by Sir Francis Dodington's Royalist cavalry. On 20 August Dodington raided Ilfracombe, and although he was driven off,[92] the threat remained.

By the time Middleton's force reached Barnstaple in late August, time had run out for Essex and his army. On 2 September the Earl's infantry surrendered, although his cavalry had escaped on 31 August. Middleton's position was now untenable. With the Barnstaple garrison rendered ineffective, he lacked the numbers to resist the advancing Royalist cavalry. On 5 September Middleton's force left Barnstaple heading for Taunton.[93] For the Royalists, Walker noted that Barnstaple was vulnerable, and '…at that time not defensible, being very unprovided of Ammunition and men.'[94]

---

87 Thomas (ed.), *The English Revolution III*, p.228.
88 Jessie Childs, *The Siege of Loyalty House a Civil War Story* (London: The Bodley Head, 2022), pp.162–164.
89 William Douglas Hamilton, *Calendar of State Papers Domestic Series of the Reign of Charles I 1644* (London: Longman and Co., 1878), pp.387–546, <http://www.british-history.ac.uk/cal-state-papers/domestic/chas1/1644/>
90 Walker, *Historical Discourses*, p.67.
91 W.G. Hoskins, *Devon*, (Chichester: Phillimore, 2003), pp.148–150. Devon roads were notoriously poor before the Turnpike era.
92 Cotton, *Barnstaple*, pp.307–310.
93 Cotton, *Barnstaple*, pp.315–316.
94 Walker, *Historical Discourses*, p.81. Walker underestimated the size of Barnstaple's garrison, but he was correct about the ammunition shortage.

Doubtless in some desperation, the Barnstaple leaders asked the Parliamentary garrison of Ilfracombe Castle for ammunition. Given the difficulties involved in supplying Barnstaple by road, it is not clear how much ammunition could have been conveyed there. In any event, it proved to be a vain hope. In the words of 'The True Informer, '…the commander in chief of the Towne [Barnstaple] sending a partie of horse for powder, they were not only denied it, but he[the Castle governor] turned his Ordnance against them, and the next day surrendered it to the King's forces.'[95]

Despite Middleton's withdrawal, Parliament remained determined to support Barnstaple. On 11 September the Commons voted to supply the town with ammunition and two days later the Committee of Both Kingdoms passed the order to Warwick.[96] Quite how the Committee expected Warwick to get the ammunition past Appledore Fort remains an open question. Fortunately perhaps, the order was over-taken by events as the Royalists overran northern Devon. According to Walker: 'GENERAL *Goring* in the interim summoned *Barnstaple*, and drew his Horse near that Town, to keep them in, who were in great Streights for want of Ammunition and other Provisions.'[97] On 17 September Barnstaple surrendered to Goring.[98]

Colonel John Luttrell continued to serve in the Parliamentary army. He was killed in a skirmish in Somerset early in 1645.[99] Colonel Sir Allen Apsley became the governor of Barnstaple and held that position for the rest of the war. After 1660 he became a prominent adherent of James Duke of York, the future James II.[100]

By the summer of 1645 it was becoming clear that the King was losing the Civil War and Prince Charles (the future Charles II) was based in Barnstaple. As noted, the Prince, doubtless accompanied by Sir Edward Hyde (the later Earl of Clarendon) and his military adviser, Sir Ralph Hopton, visited Appledore on 10 July. Although there is no documentation about this visit to Appledore Fort,

---

95   Cotton, *Barnstaple*, pp.326–327. The source quoted is *'The True Informer'*, No. 47, Sept. 21–28 1644. This journal misnames Ilfracombe Castle as 'Melcomb Castle', however a second journal, *'Perfect Occurrences of Parliament'*, Sept. 20–27 1644, correctly identifies the fort.
96   House of Commons 11 Sept. 1644 in *Journal of the House of Commons, 1643–1644* (London: His Majesty's Stationery Office,1802), vol. 3, p.624, <http://www.british-history.ac.uk/commons-jrn/vol3/pp624–625>
97   Walker, *Historical Discourses*, p.85.
98   Eugene A. Andriette, *Devon and Exeter in the Civil War* (Newton Abbot: David and Charles, 1971), p.121.
99   Sir H. C Maxwell Lyte, *a History of Dunster and the Families of Mohun and Luttrell, part II* (London: St. Catherine's Press, 1909), p.519.
100 *Dictionary of National Biography*, Apsley, Sir Allen 1616–1683, <https://doi.org/10.1093/ref:odnb/600>

clearly there was something of importance there that required a visit. The Prince was the nominal Commander of the Royalist army in the South-West and as the former commander of this army, Hopton would have been known to the Appledore garrison. Under the circumstances, the Royal party almost certainly inspected Appledore Fort.

Sir Edward Hyde, in company with the Prince of Wales, almost certainly visited Appledore Fort in 1645. ('Edward Hyde, Earl of Clarendon Lord Chancellor from an original by Gerard Soest in the National Portrait Gallery', Sir Henry Craik, frontispiece, *The Life of Edward Earl of Clarendon Lord High Chancellor of England*, (London: Smith, Elder and Co., 1911), volume 1)

On the very morning of the Prince's visit to Appledore, the New Model Army led by Sir Thomas Fairfax routed Lord Goring's Royalist Army at Langport in Somerset. The Prince and his Council had already decided to move to Cornwall and they set off for Launceston soon after the visit to Appledore. During the course of the autumn and winter, the New Model Army advanced into Devon, and besieged Exeter. On the evening of 16 February 1646, the New Model Army broke into Torrington and defeated the Royalists, now commanded once more by Hopton. The Battle of Torrington was the last major battle in the South-West.[101]

Bideford surrendered on or before 19 February when the Parliamentarians captured three ships that had sailed into the port in the mistaken belief that the Royalists were still in charge.[102] With Bideford now in Parliamentary hands, Appledore Fort was cut off from supplies and support. On 17 February Fairfax dispatched a force to watch Barnstaple,[103] and on 19 February, Commissary General Henry Ireton viewed the town and prepared quarters for a blockading force.[104] Quite possibly either Ireton, or his successor Colonel Cook,[105] decided to tighten the screw on Barnstaple by taking Appledore Fort. Even if Appledore held out, it would have surrendered along with Barnstaple on 21 April.[106]

While there is no direct evidence, it is quite possible that the Parliamentarians installed a garrison at Appledore Fort. Fairfax was concerned that the Royalists would receive support by sea. In his dispatch to the House of Commons on 19 February, Fairfax suggested that Hopton had occupied Torrington to 'secure the landing of Irish or Welch supplies so much the forwarder towards the east.'[107] This supply could only come via Appledore. Even after the Battle of Torrington, Fairfax was convinced that there could be a French landing in the West Country.[108] Fairfax certainly garrisoned Barnstaple and given his concerns about coastal security and Appledore Fort's proven ability to blockade Barnstaple, it would have made sense to garrison Appledore at the same time.

If Parliament had garrisoned Appledore Fort in 1646, this might explain why the Fort's demi-bastion and most of its ramparts have been deliberately flattened. On 25 February 1647 the *Journal of the House of Commons* recorded: 'Resolved, Xc That Salcomb Fort, Barnestable, and * *, be disgarrisoned, and the Works slighted'.[109] A garrisoned fort near Barnstaple is missing from the list of forts to be slighted.

---

101 Barratt, *Civil War*, pp.223–244.
102 Joshua Sprigg (ed.), *Anglia Rediviva; England's Recovery: being the history of the motions, actions, and successes of the army under the immediate conduct of his Excellency Sir Thomas Fairfax, KT.* (New edition, Oxford: Oxford University Press, 1854), p.205.
103 Sprigg (ed.), *Anglia Rediviva*, p.202.
104 Sprigg (ed.), *Anglia Rediviva*, p.205.
105 Cotton, *Barnstaple*, p.503.
106 Andriette, *Devon and Exeter*, pp.166–169.
107 Sprigg (ed.), *Anglia Rediviva*, p.198.
108 Sprigg (ed.), *Anglia Rediviva*, p.203.
109 *Journal of the House of Commons, 1646–1648,* 25 Feb.1647 (London: His Majesty's Stationery Office, 1802), *vol. 5,* pp.97–98,<http://www.british-history.ac.uk/commons-jrnl/

The missing fort cannot be one of the Bideford redoubts because their defences survived until the nineteenth century. Nor is it likely that the missing fort was Ilfracombe Castle because its tower appears intact in a drawing dating from 1805 and a map printed around 1870.[110] While it is impossible to prove that Appledore Fort is the missing fort, the flattening of its defences must have occurred between 1646 and the creation of the western and southern field banks, which partly overlie the earlier earthworks.

Regardless of the possible garrisoning and slighting of the Fort, Parliamentary leaders remained aware of Appledore's importance. In the spring of 1649 troops were being sent to Ireland via Appledore and the authorities were worried about a possible Irish raid. On 19 April the Council of State ordered Sir Hardress Waller to quarter some horse 'upon the Severn shore in Devon and Cornwall to protect them from the Irish rebels, and specially to take care of Appledore.'[111]

The date and function of the mound and building on the Fort site are unknown. In 2021 AC Archaeology Ltd identified later eighteenth century re-deposited glass, china and pottery fragments eroding from the mound.[112] The mound and building certainly existed by then because they appear as details in Thomas Girtin's view of Appledore painted in 1798.[113] In the early 1800s the mound was used to make sightings for the trigonometrical survey that created the first series Ordnance Survey map, although the surveyors mistook it for a 'barrow'.[114]

The original drawing for the first series Ordnance Survey map shows three objects on the site.[115] Although the drawing and the printed map are unclear, these

vol5/pp97–98/>
110 John Moore, 'Middle Ages 1154 to 1485', A History of Hele, <https://johnhmoore.co.uk/hele/middle_ages.htm.>, accessed 20 July 2023
111 Mary Anne Everett Green (ed.), *Calendar of State Papers Domestic Series (1649–1650)*, (London: Longman and Co. and Trübner and Co., 1875), p.76,<https://archive.org/details/sim_great-britain-public-record-papers-domestic-commonwealth_1649-1650/page/76/mode/2up>
112 Andrew Passmore with contributions by Richard Sims, Naomi Payne and Charlotte Coles, *Agricultural Building at Staddon Hill, Riversmeet, Appledore, Devon, (centred on NGR SS 46128 30662)* (Bardninch: AC Archaeology Ltd., 2021), pp.12–14.
113 Thomas Girtin, *View of Appledore, North Devon, from Instow Sands*, c.1798, The Courtauld Institute of Art, London, <https://www.thomasgirtin.com/collection/texts/later tours/>, accessed 2 July 2023
114 Lieutenant-Colonel William Mudge and Captain Thomas Colby, *An Account of a Trigonometrical Survey carried out by order of the Master-General of Ordnance in the years 1800, 1801, 1802, 1803, 1804, 1805, 1806, 1807, 1808 and 1809* (London: W. Bulmer and Co., 1811), p.109.
115 Barnstaple, Devon 1804, Ordnance Survey Drawings, British Library Online Gallery, UKWA, <https://www.webarchive.org.uk/wayback/archive/20090724112704/http://www.bl.uk/onlinegallery/onlineex/ordsurvdraw/b/zoomify82448.html>, accessed 2 July 2023

objects are likely to be the mound, the stone building and the east–west bank because there is no evidence of any other structures on the site at this time.[116]

Ordnance Survey original map series drawing detail. Staddon Hill is denoted 'Fort Hill' and the fort site is shown, albeit indistinctly. (Barnstaple, Devon 1804, Ordnance Survey Drawings, British Library Online Gallery, UKWA)

The mound was probably a look-out and signalling point because it is on the highest point of the hill and well-sited to offer merchants and harbour authorities in the North Devon ports advance warning of incoming ships. Such warnings were necessary in order to assemble dock workers to unload ships, especially as

116 North Devon, Sheet 26 (1:63360), Ordnance Survey, first series 1809,<https://www.visionofbritain.org.uk/maps/series?>, accessed 2 July 2023

Appledore was often used for the trans-shipment of cargoes to Barnstaple.[117] In 1841 a tower was built 900 metres from the fort site to warn Bideford of incoming ships.[118] In the mid-nineteenth century the mound was briefly used as the base for an Admiralty storm warning flagstaff.[119]

The building probably post-dates the mound because it would have partly obscured the view of the sea from the mound. In Girtin's painting the building is partly hidden by a tree and its eastern side appears roofless and windowless. The lack of chimneys and wide entrance suggest it was an agricultural building, possibly a barn for animals, rather than a dwelling. The building appears in later nineteenth century maps but it is not mentioned in Cotton's account of the earthworks. By 1922 only some low walls and a higher fragment of the north wall remained.[120]

Despite its obvious defensible position overlooking the waterways to Barnstaple and Bideford, the Fort site was not used again for defensive purposes. An inaccurate French map of 1768 appears to show a tower on Staddon Hill,[121] but the tower was actually 300 metres south-west of the Fort site. A map dating from the 1870s shows this tower's location and denotes it as 'Look Out'.[122] The tower was demolished in the 1950s but its exterior and internal fittings reportedly resembled a mid-eighteenth century gazebo tower in Torrington.[123]

There were proposals for a new fort on Staddon Hill in 1859,[124] and again in 1893,[125] but no fortifications were ever built. Throughout the twentieth century the Fort site remained in agricultural use and from the 1950s to the 1980s there was a piggery against the northern bank.[126] In 2022 Appledore Fort was recognised as

117 Carter, *Illustrated History 3*, p.43; p.53, p.104.
118 Basil Greenhill and Anne Giffard, *Westcountrymen in Prince Edward's Isle: a fragment of the great migration* (Halifax NS, Canada: Formac Publishing Co. Ltd., 2003), p119.
119 Janet and Peter Keene, *Northam Burrows estuary environments* (Kingston Bagpuize: Thematic Trails, 1997), p.3.
120 *Appledore from the Air,* 1922 aerial photograph of Appledore in Peter Christie and Pat Slade, *Appledore, Northam and Westward Ho! Through the Lens, Part 1* (Bideford: 2011), p.8.
121 David Carter, *Illustrated History of Appledore* (Appledore: David Carter, 2000), vol. 1, p.30; p.46.
122 *c*.1870 Map of Northam in Carter, *Illustrated History 3*, rear cover.
123 Witness Statement: Mrs Jenny Arnold in Arnold, *Historical and Archaeological Report*, p.4. The gazebo is described in Historic England, Palmer House including garden wall, List entry 1104777<http://historicengland.org.uk/listing/the-list/list-entry/11104777>, accessed 19 May 2021
124 *North Devon Journal,* 7 April 1859.
125 *North Devon Journal,* 26 Jan. 1893.
126 Gent, *Archaeological Observations*, p.1.

being of national importance and the site became a scheduled ancient monument.[127] It is worth spelling out the nature of that significance.

Contemporary military experts were correct to anticipate that small redoubts could control communications and annoy enemy forces. During the Civil War in other contested areas such as the West Midlands a network of fieldworks also protected towns and larger forts, controlled territories and resources and collected intelligence. Unsurprisingly, these small redoubts were often the focus of inter-garrison skirmishes and raiding.[128]

Although Appledore Fort fits into this general pattern, its particular importance depended on its control of the riverine access to Bideford and Barnstaple rather than any direct control over a hinterland or land communications. The Fort was intended to be part of a system of forts that protected Bideford and the access to Barnstaple. In the event, Appledore Fort proved to be the key to the whole system and therefore the key to securing the North Devon ports. For this reason, after 1644 Appledore Fort ensured Royalist control of northern Devon for the rest of the war. It is ironic that a fort built by Parliament should prove so valuable to their opponents.

Although evidently a small fort, Appledore Fort attracted the attention of leaders such as Prince Maurice and Charles I in 1644. It was deemed important enough for Parliamentary forces to besiege and for the Royalists to relieve, while risking the security of Exeter. In short, Appledore Fort's strategic location enabled it to play a role out of all proportion to its small size.

The successful defence of Appledore Fort and its relief on 20 August 1644 were remarkable achievements with real consequences for the campaign in the South-West. With hindsight it is clear that Sir John Middleton's chances of disrupting the Royalist campaign in Cornwall required the assistance of the Barnstaple garrison. In the event, the King's decision to weaken the Exeter garrison and temporarily risk his lines of communication to relieve the Fort proved to be the right choice. By keeping the Barnstaple garrison inactive, Appledore Fort guaranteed Middleton's failure and helped to safeguard the Royalist lines of communication for the remainder of the campaign, thereafter ensuring the rapid surrender of Barnstaple and northern Devon to the Royalist forces. In this way, the successful defence of the Fort made a tangible contribution to the King's greatest victory.

Although the Fort is damaged, enough of its earthworks and their setting survive to enable the defences and their history to be understood. In particular,

---

127 Historic England, Civil War Fieldwork on Staddon Hill 1476886: Official list entry, <https://historicengland.org.uk/listing/the-list/list-entry/1476886?section=official-list-entry>, accessed 17 June 2023

128 Jonathan Worton, "Coursing the Tinkerley Fox': tactics of garrison warfare in the West Midlands during 1643 and 1644", *Midland History*, 47:1 (2022), pp.44–46.

the two fields in which the Fort is located and the estuarine views to the north are largely unchanged, enabling the visitor to readily grasp the reason for the Fort's location and witness the same ever-changing tides and weather that the garrison experienced. At such moments it is easy to appreciate the desperate situation of the 40 musketeers who, in the face of overwhelming odds in the summer of 1644, absolutely refused to surrender their Fort – and won.

Appledore Fort site looking north. The estuarine views in this direction have altered little since the Civil War period. (Author's photo)

Bibliography

Maps

Ordnance Survey, Barnstaple, Devon 1804, Ordnance Survey Drawings, British Library Online Gallery, UKWA, <https://www.webarchive.org.uk/wayback/archive/20090724112704/http://www.bl.uk/onlinegallery/onlineex/ordsurvdraw/b/zoomify82448.html>, accessed 2 July 2023

Ordnance Survey First Series, Sheet 26, Barnstaple, <https://www.visionofbritain.org.uk/maps/series?>, accessed 2 July 2023

Tithe Map of Bideford 1841, <https://maps.bristol.gov.uk/kyp?edition=devon&mapbse=2017>, accessed 19 May 2021

Tithe Map of Northam 1839, <https://maps.bristol.gov.uk/kyp?edition=devon&mapbse=2017>, accessed 19 May 2021

Primary Sources

Bideford Tithe Apportionments (transcript), <https://www.devon.gov.uk/historicenvironment/tithe-map/bideford/>, accessed 19 May 2021

Clarendon, Earl of, *The History of the Rebellion and Civil War in England begun in the year 1641* (Oxford: Clarendon Press, 1888), volume 3.

Green, Mary Anne Everett (ed.), *Calendar of State Papers Domestic Series, 1649–1650*, (London: Longman and Co. and Trübner and Co., 1875), p.76, <https://archive.org/details/sim_great-britain-public-record-papers-domestic-commonwealth_1649–1650/page/76/mode/2up>, accessed 17 June 2023

Defoe, Daniel, *A tour thro' the whole island of Great Britain, divided into circuits or journies, Letter IV Containing a description of the north shore of the counties of Cornwall, and Devon, and some parts of Somersetshire, Wiltshire, Dorsetshire, Gloucestershire, Buckinghamshire and Berkshire* (London: J. M. Dent and Co., 1927), <https://www.visionofbritain.org.uk/travellers/Defoe/15>

Hamilton, William Douglas, *Calendar of State Papers, Domestic Series of the Reign of Charles I, 1639–1640* (London: Longman and Co., 1877), vol. 15, pp.66–116, <http://www.british-history.ac.uk/cal-state-papers/domestic/chas1/1639-40/>, accessed 19 May 2021

Hamilton, William Douglas, *Calendar of State Papers Domestic Series of the Reign of Charles I 1644*, (London: Longman and Co., 1878), pp.387–546, <http://www.british-history.ac.uk/cal-state-papers/domestic/chas1/1644/>, accessed 19 May 2021

Journal of the House of Commons, 1643–1644 (London 1802), vol. 3, p.624, 11 September 1644 <http://www.british-history.ac.uk/commons-jrn/vol3/pp624-625>, accessed 19 May 2021

Journal of the House of Commons, 1646–1648, (London: His Majesty's Stationery Office, 1802), *vol. 5, 25 February 1647,* pp.97–98,
<http://www.british-history.ac.uk/commons-jrnl/vol5/pp97-98/>, accessed 9 Sept. 2021

Hexham, Henry, *The Principles of the Art Military, as practised in the warres of the United Netherlands, Part 2,* (Delft: Jan Pieters Walpote, 1638)

Mudge, Lieutenant-Colonel William and Colby, Captain Thomas, *An Account of a Trigonometrical Survey carried out by order of the Master-General of His Majesty's Ordnance in the years 1800, 1801, 1802, 1803, 1804, 1805, 1806, 1807, 1808 and 1809,* (London: W. Bulmer and Co., 1811)

Northam Burials 1538–1649,
<http://www.genuki.org.uk/big/eng/DEV/Northam/NorthamBurials1538-1649>, accessed 19 May 2021

North Devon Journal, 7 April 1859

North Devon Journal, 26 Jan. 1893

Sprigg, Joshua (ed.), *Anglia Rediviva; England's Recovery* (New edition, Oxford: Oxford University Press, 1854)

Thomas, P. (ed.), *The English Revolution III: Oxford Royalist* (London: Cornmarket Press 1971)

May 2021; *Northam Tithe Map Index,*
<http://www.genuki.org.uk/big/eng/DEV/Northam/NorthamTithes>, accessed 19May 2021

Walker, Sir Edward, *Historical Discourses upon Several Occasions,* (London: Sam. Keble, 1705)

Ward, Robert, *Animadversions of Warre or, a militarie magazine of the truest rules and ablest instructions for the managing of warre,* (London: John Dawson, 1639)

Secondary Sources

Andriette, Eugene A., *Devon and Exeter in the Civil War,* (Newton Abbot: David and Charles, 1971)

Arnold, Nick, *Historical and Archaeological Report: Appledore Fort, Staddon Hill, Appledore, Devon,* (unpublished, 2021)

Ascott, Major W., *Random Notes of Old Bideford and District,* (Bideford: Bideford Gazette, 1953)

Barratt, John, *Civil War in the South-West: 1642–1646* (Barnsley: Pen and Sword Books Ltd, 2005)

Barratt, John, *Sieges of the English Civil War,* (Barnsley: Pen and Sword Books, 2008)

Carter, David, *Illustrated History of Appledore,* (Appledore: David Carter, 2000), vol. 1

Carter, David, Illustrated History of Appledore: its place in history, (Appledore: David Carter, 2017), vol. 3

Childs, Jessie, *The Siege of Loyalty House a Civil War Story*, (London: The Bodley Head, 2022)

Christie, Peter and Slade, Pat, *Appledore, Northam and Westward Ho! Through the Lens, Part 1*, (Bideford: 2011)

Cotton, Richard W., *Barnstaple and Northern Part of Devon during the Great Civil War 1642–1646*, (London: Unwin Brothers, 1889)

Devon and Dartmoor Historic Environment Record MDV11870 – Civil War Fort on Staddon Hill, Northam, <http://www.heritagegateway.org.uk/gateway/Results-Single.aspx?uid=MDV11870&resourceID=104>, accessed 19 May 2021

Dictionary of National Biography, Apsley, Sir Allen 1616–1683, <https://doi.org/10.1093/ref:odnb/600>, accessed 19 May 2021

Dictionary of National Biography, Chudleigh, James 1617–1643, <https://doi.org/10.1093/ref:odnb/5382>, accessed 19 May 2021

Edwards, Mark, *An Archaeological Magnetometer Survey, Land at Staddon Hill, Appledore Centred on NGR: 246125, 130677 Report: 2104APP-R-1*, (Bideford, Substrata Ltd., 2021)

Gent, T. H., *Archaeological Observations at Staddon Hill, Appledore*, (Exeter: Exeter Archaeology, 1995), Devon and Dartmoor Historic Environment Record MDV11870 – Civil War Fort on Staddon Hill, Northam

Greenhill, Basil and Giffard, Anne, *Westcountrymen in Prince Edward's Isle: a fragment of the great migration*, (Halifax NS, Canada: Formac Publishing Co. Ltd., 2003)

Harrington, Peter, *English Civil War Fortifications 1642–1651*, (Oxford: Osprey, 2003)

Historic England, Civil War Fieldwork on Staddon Hill 1476886: Official list entry, Historic England <https://historicengland.org.uk/listing/the-list/list-entry/1476886?section=official-list-entry>, accessed 17 June 2023

Historic England, Civil War redoubt 680 m north west of Dairy Farm 10168048: Official list entry, Historic England, <https://historicengland.org.uk/listing/the-list/list-entry/1016048?section=official-list-entry>, accessed 8 June 2023

Historic England, Palmer House including garden wall, List entry 1104777 <http://historicengland.org.uk/listing/the-list/list-entry/11104777>, accessed 19 May 2021

Historic England, The Folly including boundary walls on north and south sides 1200932: Official list entry, <https://historicengland.org.uk/listing/the-list/list-entry/1200932?section=official-list-entry>, accessed 16 June 2023

Hoskins, W. G., *Devon* (Chichester: Phillimore and Co., 2003), pp.148–150

Keene, Janet and Peter, *Northam Burrows estuary environments*, (Kingston Bagpuize: Thematic Trails, 1997)

Maxwell Lyte, Sir H. C, *A History of Dunster and the families of Mohun and Luttrell, part II* (London: St. Catherine's Press, 1909)

Moore, John, 'Middle Ages 1154 to 1485', A History of Hele, <https://johnhmoore.co.uk/hele/middle_ages.htm.>, accessed 20 July 2023

Northcote, Lady Rosalind, *Devon Its Moorland, Streams and Coasts*, (London: Chatto and Windus, 1908)

Passmore, Andrew with contributions by Sims, Richard, Payne, Naomi and Coles, Charlotte, *Agricultural Building at Staddon Hill, Riversmeet, Appledore, Devon, (centred on NGR SS 46128 30662)*, (Bardninch: AC Archaeology Ltd., 2021)

Watkins, John, *A History of Bideford in the County of Devon*, (Bideford: Edward Gaskell Publishers, 1993)

William White, History, *Gazetteer, and Directory of Devonshire and the city and county of the city of Exeter comprising a general survey of the county of Devon and the diocese of Exeter* (Sheffield: Robert Leader, 1850)

Worton, Jonathan, "Coursing the Tinkerley Fox': Tactics of Garrison Warfare in the West Midlands during 1643 and 1644', *Midland History*, 47:1 (2022), pp.44–46

The Civil War Defences and Siegeworks of Oxford

David Radford

The Royalist defences around Oxford were established in 1642 when Charles I made the city his temporary capital and base of operations. The defences were added to until 1646 when the garrison surrendered to Parliamentarian forces. A number of archaeological investigations over the last 20 years have added to our understanding of the both the defences and the Parliamentarian siegeworks, though the full extent and character of the military works remains to be established. This article provides a summary of these investigations.

Topological and Historical Context

Oxford sits on a terrace of gravel with rivers and floodplains to the east, west and south making it easily defendable by damning the rivers and flooding the water meadows. The gently sloping northern approach along the gravel terrace would have been far more vulnerable to attack and required stout defences. At the outbreak of hostilities in August 1642 a pro-Royalist militia of scholars and servants, assembled by the acting Pro Vice Chancellor of the University Dr Pinke, threw up defences across the approach roads and may have attempted to construct a rapid line of defences north of the city between the Thames (Isis) and Cherwell rivers.[1] These initial efforts were thrown down by a Parliamentarian force that briefly occupied the city in September 1642. The King arrived to take up residence

---

1   The proposals for a defensive line were the subject of a heated debate between Sir Richard Cave who was advising the University on possible fortifications and the local MPs who had Parliamentary leanings and 'line with redoubts and a foot-pace' was discussed, this is detailed in H.M.C. Portland Mss. I. pp.59–63. See also R. T. Lattey, E. J. S. Parsons and I. G. Philip. 'A Contemporary Map of the Defences of Oxford in 1644', in *Oxoniensia*, 1, (1936), p.66 and John Barratt, *Cavalier Capital: Oxford in the English Civil War 1642–1646*, (Solihull, Helion & Company Ltd, 2015).

at Christ Church in November and between the winter of 1642 and the summer of 1646 Royalist forces oversaw the construction of a more robust defensive arrangement[2].

No detailed written records relating to the construction of the defences have survived, although there are some references in the *Royalist Ordnance Papers* and a number casual observations made by Royalist and Parliamentarian officers and other observers that provide some clues to their evolution.[3] The diarist and antiquarian Anthony Wood made a number of observations regarding the defences, although he was only a schoolboy at the time.[4]

A map by Sir Bernard de Gomme (1620–85), an engineer working in the service of Prince Rupert, dated to 1644 though with the date 1645 crossed out, shows the likely layout of the defensive lines. However, it is unclear whether all of the forts and ramparts shown were built as depicted. After the Civil War much of the defensive system, comprising booms across the rivers, large banks of earth, dry and wet ditches, lines of storm poles, palisades and pit falls, was slighted and the remaining earthworks were slowly denuded by farming, gardening and the expansion of college and University buildings. Parts of the defences are shown on seventeenth to nineteenth century maps as they were slowly enveloped by the expanding northern suburb of Oxford. Some caution is needed in interpreting these maps as some sections of the Royalist rampart were already incorporated into formalised college garden schemes by the time of first available post-Civil War map by David Loggan, dated c1678, perhaps having been refashioned to suit the garden fashions of the time. Furthermore, some sections of earthen banks shown on Loggan's map appear never to have formed part of the defences and likely originated as garden features.[5]

---

2   For a summary of the usefulness of the historic maps associated with the defences see Anthony Kemp 'The Fortification of Oxford during the Civil War', in *Oxoniensia*, 42 (1977), p.245. For a recent summary of the defences and detailed map of identified parts of the Royalist lines see Julian Munby 'Note on Oxford's Civil War Earthworks' in Alan Crossley (ed.), *British Historic Towns Atlas Volume VII Oxford Introduction and Gazetteer*, (The Historic Town Trust, 2021), pp.55–56. and Map 8 Sheet N.
3   For a summary of these references see Frederick J. Varley *The Siege of Oxford: An Account of Oxford During the Civil War, 1642–1646* (Oxford: Oxford University Press, 1932); Frederick J. Varley *Supplement to the siege of Oxford* (Oxford: Oxford University Press, 1935); Lattey et al, *A Contemporary Map*; Kemp 'The Fortification of Oxford',pp.237–246.; John Barratt, *Cavalier Capital*, pp.74–79.
4   Anthony à Wood (Andrew Clark ed.), *The Life and Times of Anthony Wood, Antiquary of Oxford, 1632–1695, described by himself* (Oxford: OUP, 1891), Volume I.
5   For example, the north-south bank depicted at St John's College fronting onto Parks Road. Likewise, the origins of the intramural bank or rampart built up against the city wall at Merton College is also unknown.

Oxford's medieval walls had seen a major period of strengthening and rebuilding in the thirteenth century only to be rapidly compromised by the siting of religious precincts adjacent or, as in the case of the Augustinian Cannons at St Frideswide's and the Greyfriars, across the line of the city wall. Like other English towns Oxford had never felt the need for up-to-date earthwork defences capable of withstanding cannon fire. Nevertheless, the Royalist occupation did see the strengthening of the remaining lines of medieval walls, with the de Gomme map suggesting that at least the coherent sections of standing wall in the eastern part of the city were considered part of the defensive lines.[6]

In 1642 it would have been possible to go to the Bodleian Library and examine books on contemporary Continental defensive systems, equally there were men in the Kings service who had served in European wars and had knowledge of modern defensive systems.[7] A young mathematician, Richard Rallingson, at The Queen's College was rewarded by the King for coming up with an elaborate plan for the defence of the city involving a Dutch style tenaille trace system of which there is a surviving plan.[8] However, the defences were not completed to this design, although there are some similarities. In fact, the inner defensive line shown on de Gomme's map as a thin line, does not follow clear military principles regarding requirements for flanking fire, but appears to make use of existing landscape features and college boundaries. This is assumed to be either a line established by the Chancellor of the University or a scheme conceived by one of the King's officers, perhaps Sir Charles Lloyd (c.1602–61) who was the King's Chief Engineer, and commenced in late 1642 or early 1643.[9] The inner line is described as 'not finished' near Gloucester Hall (Worcester College) by Sir Samuel Luke in March 1642[10] and is assumed to have been completed by August 1643 by which time it was armed with ordnance.[11] It was observed by the Parliamentarian Sir William Waller in July 1644 when he noted that 'the whole north side [of the town is] palisaded'.[12]

Once the King had established his residence and royal officers were in command the substantive work on the inner line was undertaken by work parties formed by

---

6   This is discussed further below.
7   Kemp *The Fortification of Oxford*, p.242.
8   For a discussion of Rallingson's role in the defences see Lattey et al, *A Contemporary Map*, pp.161–164 and fig 25., Kemp *The Fortification of Oxford*, pp.238–240; William Poole, 'A royalist mathematical practitioner in interregnum Oxford: the exploits of Richard Rawlinson (1616–1668)', in *The Seventeenth Century*, (online journal, 2018).
9   Barratt, *Cavalier Capital*, p.78.
10 *The Journal of Sir Samuel Luke. Scoutmaster-General to the Earl of Essex.* (Oxford: Oxford Records Society, 1947), pp.34–5.
11 Ian Roy (ed.), *The Royalist Ordnance Papers*, (Oxford: Oxfordshire Records Society 1964 & 1975), note 19, 468, B145. B156 & B168.
12 *Calendar of State Papers Domestic Series 1644*, p.363.

levies of able bodied townsfolk.[13] A notable feature of the inner most northern defensive rampart line as shown by de Gomme is that it runs eastwards to meet the walled precinct of Magdalen College and thus excludes the suburb of Holywell which was owned by Merton College, the only college to have expressed Parliamentarian sympathies.[14]

There are short documentary references to improvements to the defences which are not definitive but allow for a broad framework to be suggested involving the strengthening of the inner line between 1643–4 and the creation and improvement of an outer line using a more militarily robust tenaille trace system between 1644 and 1646. Kemp suggests that the outer line was a response to the Royalist defeat at Naseby in June 1645, after which it became clear that Oxford would soon be a renewed target,[15] with de Gomme being the most likely candidate to have been the architect of the outer works.[16] In 1646, Sir Thomas Fairfax noted two lines of defence and 'many material improvement' since his last visit in 1645, implying the substantive works for the outer line post-date the summer of 1645 when he was previously at Oxford.[17] Additionally, in Sir William Waller's report of 1644 he noted that Oxford was 'much stronger fortified' but makes no mention of a double line of defences.[18]

In 1644 an initial attempt to entrap the King in the City failed when the two Parliamentarian armies led by the Earl of Essex and Sir William Waller failed to coordinate and Charles escaped across Port Meadow to the north of the city with a sizeable body of men. Subsequently, a short siege in 1645 and longer siege in 1646 were overseen by Sir Thomas Fairfax for the Parliamentarians. In 1645 Fairfax established a camp and initial siege lines on Headington Hill and these were expanded in 1646.[19] De Gomme maps the main eastern line of siegeworks but with little annotation to landmarks. Elsewhere there is some archaeological evidence for further unmapped Parliamentarian lines – these are discussed further below. The Privy Council surrendered the City in June 1646 and the defences were slighted between 1647 and 1648. The Parliamentarian Governor, Colonel Draper, was then

---

13 Lattey, et al, *A Contemporary Map*, p.168.
14 Ian Roy and Dietrich Reinhart 'Oxford and the Civil Wars' in Nicholas Tyacke (ed.) *The History of the University of Oxford: Volume IV Seventeenth Century* (Oxford: Oxford University Press, 1997), p.712.
15 Kemp, 'The Fortification of Oxford', p.244.
16 Andrew Saunders, *Fortress Builder. Bernard de Gomme, Charles II's Military Engineer*, (Exeter: University of Exeter Press, 2004), pp.70–73.
17 Kemp, 'The Fortification of Oxford', p.244. Report to the Council of War on 3 May 1646 in J. Madan, A *Catalogue of Oxford Books* (Oxford: Clarendon Press, 1912), note 38, II, item 1892.
18 *Calendar of State Papers Domestic: Charles I, 1644*, 363.
19 Lattey, et al, A Contemporary Map; C.S.P.D., p.406.

ordered to refortify the castle between 1650 and 1651, however these works were slighted in July or August 1651 following the invasion of the Scots and anticipating the arrival of Charles II.[20]

The Medieval City Wall and Ditch

De Gomme's map clearly inks in the eastern walled circuit of the medieval city wall as it runs around New College and Merton College and the implication is that in this area at least the wall retained some functional utility. An outer or concentric city wall line had been added to the north-east quadrant of the circuit, probably in the later thirteenth century, built along the inner lip of the city ditch on the edge of the berm. This outer line is ambiguously represented on maps on late seventeenth century maps leading Brian Durham to suggest that it may have also been brought back into use during the Civil War although the most recent archaeological evidence does not support this.[21]

In terms of the surviving physical evidence it has been suggested that crude holes cut through medieval arrow slits in the bastion north of New College chapel may be Civil War firing positions.[22] Elsewhere archaeological investigations of the city ditch around the northern and eastern city wall line at No.39 George Street, Hertford College, the Bodleian link tunnel and New College have all produced evidence for a deep post-medieval recut which is assumed to relate to Royalist efforts to revive the medieval defences.[23] At New College the excavator suggested that one motivation for the location of the recut may have been to rob the buried outer medieval wall for stone to use for repairs to the primary medieval city wall.[24] Between the Northgate and Smithgate it is unclear whether the medieval city wall remained defendable at the time of the conflict as it appears to be heavily compromised by buildings on Loggan's 1675 Map.[25]

20 Julian Munby, Andrew Norton, Dan Poore and Anne Dodd *Excavations at Oxford Castle 1999–2009* (York: Thames Valley Landscapes Monograph No.44, 2019), p.169–170.; Tom G. Hassall, 'Excavations at Oxford Castle, 1965–1973', in *Oxoniensia*, 41 (1976), p.247.
21 Brian Durham, Claire Halpin, Nicholas Palmer, 'Oxford's Northern Defences; Archaeological Studies', in *Oxoniensia*, 48 (1983), p.39.
22 Kemp, 'The Fortification of Oxford', p.242.
23 Durham, et al, 'Oxford's Northern Defences', p.19.
24 Robin Bashford, *New College, Longwall Street Archaeological Evaluation Report* (Unpublished Oxford Archaeology Report 2015), pp.18–19.
25 Durham has suggested that this pattern of building is a result of a major change in landownership in this area between 1640 and 1649 that resulted in the partial dismantling and development of the wall and ditch plots in this area after the war. Recent work at the former 'Boswell's Department Store' basement located east of the Northgate found no evidence of a deep seventeenth century recut of the city ditch and it is possible that

The Colleges

In 1642 Oxford had numerous walled precincts belonging to the University, colleges and former religious institutions that could be utilised for military and related manufacturing purposes.[26] There is little visible physical evidence for Royalist modification of these spaces.[27] A large designed garden feature, the New College mound, is likely to have been adapted as an observation platform, and perhaps less likely as a firing platform. *The Journal of Sir Samuel Luke* notes that on 16 March 1643, 'There is a mount made in the Colledge, about six score within the works. Against Wadham Colledge there is a mount cast uppe where there is two peeces of ordinance, but the works are not finished.'[28] The 33 metre square and 15 metre high New College mound was investigated in 1993 and found to contain pottery consistent with a sixteenth century construction date. Mid-seventeenth century clay pipes were found at the top which appeared to have been truncated, possibly in the eighteenth century.[29] The location of the mound referred to by Luke at Wadham College is not known.

The Northern Defences – The Inner Line

The first and inner line of northern defences is depicted by de Gomme as a thin line and can be traced from the east bank of the Castle Mill Stream opposite the walled precinct of Rewley Abbey through the grounds of Gloucester Hall (later Worcester College) towards Walton Street. De Gomme's map indicates that no later outer line was added to very western section of the defences east of the Castle Mill Stream, perhaps suggesting the ability to partially flood the area to the north. The inner line runs through Exeter College Cohen Quadrangle, formerly Ruskin Hall, where in 2015 a watching brief undertaken during the extension of the cellar revealed an east–west ditch that survived to *c.*4.5 metres wide and 1.3 metres deep.

---

this section was already too compromised by buildings placed against the wall to make clearance viable (Pers. Obs.). For the infilling of the city ditch and built up character between the North Gate and Smith Gate see E. T. Leeds 'note' in J. Daniell, 'The City Wall and Ditch in the Clarendon Quadrangle', in *Oxoniensia*, 4, 1939, p.159.

26   A review of the standing buildings repurposed for the Royalist occupation is outside the scope of this paper. For a summary of functions assigned to different colleges see Barratt xxxx.

27   For an article on the King's gate at Christ Church see https://www.chch.ox.ac.uk/blog/king-charles-gate-advent-doors-2018.

28   *The Journal of Sir Samuel Luke. Scoutmaster-General to the Earl of Essex.* (Oxford: Oxford Records Society, 1947), pp.34–35.

29   Chris Bell, *New College Mound, Oxford: An Archaeological Investigation* (Unpublished Oxford Archaeological Unit Report, 1993)

The lower fills were waterlogged and it may have originated as one of a series of drainage channels shown on cartographic sources pre-dating the construction of the defences in the mid-seventeenth century.[30]

As the inner line turns north up through the modern Wellington Square, enclosing what used to be Gloucester Green, the alignment becomes almost curvilinear. The line is captured as a surviving earthwork on Loggan's map and perhaps corresponds to a pre-existing earthwork boundary around Gloucester Green (or Broken Hayes). The line then extends around St Giles's Church and appears to form a simple hornwork protecting the Woodstock and Banbury Roads.

A section of rampart belonging to the inner northern Royalist defensive line at Wadham College Fellow's Garden. (Author's photograph)

---

30   Both de Gomme and Loggan show a complex arrangement of drainage or irrigation channels in this area, perhaps linked to market gardening, and it is possible that defences utilised pre-existing features in some way. See Robin Bashford, 'Exeter College, Ruskin Building, Walton Street, Oxford: Archaeological Watching Brief', (unpublished OA report, 2015)

East of the Banbury Road the line of defences heads south-east towards the northern boundary of Rhodes House. The inner line between Rhodes House and Mansfield Road to the east is the only section of the defences that survives as a substantive earthwork above ground. However, it is not without its interpretative challenges. By the late seventeenth century some of the earthworks in this area had in part been converted into garden features and the possibility that they have been altered over time cannot be discounted. In 1979 a watching brief during works to a garden feature in the rampart east of Rhodes House revealed a lens of gravel overlain by dumped soil and loam that contained demolition debris from a stone wall. The recorded interpretation on the Historic Environment Records (HER) suggests that the bank was of Civil War date but a subsequent interpretation questions this.[31]

Loggan's map diverges from the de Gomme map in showing a large defensive bank and ditch heading northwards from the eastern end of what is now Rhodes House, linking up with the later outer defensive line. He also shows a smaller bank heading west at this point from the north-east corner of the current Rhodes House, which is generally accepted to be the route of the inner line.[32]

An excavation in the grounds of Rhodes House by Museum of London Archaeology (MOLA) in 2020–21 revealed an east–west 'V' shaped ditch either side of Rhodes House containing seventeenth century material and measuring up to 3.4 metres in width and 1.38 metres in depth, with a possibly contemporary slot-like feature running parallel to the north.[33] Unexpectedly, this was located to the south of the projected east–west line shown by Loggan and the ditch could therefore be an initial line that was subsequently rationalised northwards or alternatively evidence that the sequence is more complicated than depicted on available maps.[34]

To the east of Rhodes House an earthwork bank survives heading south through into Wadham Fellows Garden, then running eastwards as a landscaped bank along the boundary of Mansfield College and the recently built New College

---

31   Oxford HER No EOX4962; Oxford Notebooks No 5 (Oxford Archaeological Unit Archive). Brian Durham later states that the current bank material may be no earlier than eighteenth century in this location Durham et al, 1983 op. cit. note 89, though this could relate to a localised remodelling of the bank.

32   On Taylor's 1750 map this east–west earthwork enclosing the garden at its northern end is shown and labelled 'Part of the Old Fortifications'. The northward extension is not shown but corresponds to a trackway and arable field division.

33   Pers. Comm., P. Clemente; MOLA forthcoming.

34   Wood says of this area in December 1642, 'I went to see the trenches then digging and making about the old trench that was formerly made by the scholars at the end of the wall of St John's college walks'. Wood Life and Times, p.72)

A section through a likely Civil War defensive ditch at Rhodes House, looking east. (Courtesy of Museum of London Archaeology)

Gradel Quadrangles.[35] The outer ditch along this section has been infilled but has been excavated on several occasions. Between the Parks Road and Magdalen Deer Park the inner line ditch has been investigated at Rhodes House, the American Institute, Mansfield College, the University Club and at Balliol College Sports Field.[36] At the American Institute a parallel narrow gully and a line of post-holes

---

35   Here de Gomme's line is less acute that Loggan's, if extrapolated onto modern maps it should run north-east to south-west through the grounds of Mansfield College however sufficient archaeological excavation has taken place in this area to discount this route: See A. Simmonds et. al., 2020, op. cit., fig 13.1 and Alan Crossley (ed.), *The British Historic Town Atlas Volume VII Oxford* (Historic Towns Trust & Oxford Archaeology 2021), Sheet N.

36   Excavations at Rhodes House MOLA forthcoming; Paul Booth and Chris Hayden, 'A Roman Settlement at Mansfield Road, Oxford', in *Oxoniesia*, 65 (2000), pp.291–331; OAU (no author) 'Oxford, Mansfield College: Evaluation Report' (Unpublished Oxford Archaeological Unit Report, 1992); Adam Brossler, 'New University Club House, Mansfield Road, Oxford Archaeological Watching Brief Report' (Unpublished OAU report, 2003),

recorded east of, and outside of, the inner line ditch may have formed part of an additional defensive works.[37] Excavations at New College Music Room by OA in 2015 and at New College School by MOLA in 2019–20 investigated the make-up of the rampart of the inner line. In both locations it was found to be constructed using stacked turves with tips of gravel above, although there is no definitive dating for the turf bank and it may be an earlier feature.[38] David Sturdy has previously suggested the presence of a Late Saxon defensive earthwork along this line.[39]

A section of sieved spits across the turf rampart at New College School, Oxford. (Courtesy of Museum of London Archaeology)

Steven Teague, 'Balliol College Recreation Ground, Jowett Walk, Oxford Post-Excavation Assessment', (unpublished Oxford Archaeology Report, 2020); Steve Teague & Ben Ford, 'New College Music Room' and Paulo Clemente & R. Clare 'New College Savile Road'.
37 Booth and Hayden, 'A Roman Settlement at Mansfield Road', Oxford, p.306.
38 Steve Teague and Ben Ford 'The Civil War Earthwork and Earlier Remains at Savile House, New College, Mansfield Rd, Oxford', (Oxford Archaeology Draft Publication Report, 2020); Paulo Clemente and Rachel Clare 'New College Savile Road Oxford Post-Excavation Assessment and Updated Project Design', (Museum of London Archaeology unpublished report, 2021).
39 David Sturdy, *Historic Oxford* (Stroud: Tempus 2004), p.29 & fig. 11.

A section of the outer ditch belonging to the inner northern Royalist defensive line at Mansfield College. (Courtesy of Oxford Archaeology)

The adjacent ditch was excavated at Mansfield College to the north by OA in 2016. It was not fully sectioned; the excavated section was 7 metres wide and up to 1.8 metres deep with steep sides and a flat base. Notably, it had been recut in the seventeenth century with the north face of the recut located around 2 metres south of the corresponding slope of the original ditch; the recut ditch measuring at least 3.3 metres wide and 1.25 metres deep.[40] There was no certain evidence of waterlogging in the basal fills of the ditch.

The turf constructed bank and initial ditch could therefore potentially be an initial line established by the University militia that was subsequently slighted by the Parliamentarians and recut under the direction of the King's officers, however there remain uncertainties relating to the dating of the turf rampart and it may have been a pre-existing feature that was opportunistically incorporated into the inner line.[41]

---

40 Andrew Simmonds et al, 'Roman Settlement and the North-Eastern Civil War Defences of Oxford: Investigations at Mansfield College and the Tinbergen Building' in A. Dodd, S. Mileson and L. Webley, *The Archaeology of Oxford in the 21st Century Investigations in the City by Oxford Archaeology 2006–16* (OAHS Occasional Paper 1, 2020), p.443.
41 Steve Teague and Ben Ford 'The Civil War Earthwork and Earlier Remains at Savile House'; Paulo Clemente and Rachel Clare, 'New College Savile Road Oxford'; Simmonds et al, 'Roman Settlement and the North-Eastern Civil War Defences of Oxford', p.440;

East of Mansfield Road a 'V' shaped redan or emplacement of the inner line survives as a heavily landscaped earthwork south of the University Club. Just to the east of this a partial section of the inner ditch excavated in 2003 produced further evidence for a recut of the inner line ditch.[42] To the east of this the inner line runs south below the re-landscaped Balliol College Cricket Field towards Holywell. Further east at Balliol College Sports Field, excavations in 2018–19 showed the inner line approached St Cross Road slightly to the north of the fifteenth century wall of Magdalen College. Here the ditch was sectioned and found to be 6 metres wide and 2.5 metres deep and had steep 45 degree sides and a concave base. It contained a series of fills indicating deliberate backfilling, though no recut was identified.[43] A further section through the ditch was reported just to the south when digging a cellar for houses for Balliol College on Jowett Walk in 1960.[44]

The Northern Outer Line

The northern outer line was established on a much clearer set of military principles following the tenaille trace system, a Continental system of banks and ditches creating a zigzag pattern of alternating projecting salients with cannon positions providing enfilading fire across adjacent recesses or re-entrants. The full Dutch system would have demanded a more complex arrangement of inner and outer defences and covered walkway, the defenders appear to have been pragmatic and simply added the outer designed envelope to the cruder inner line.[45] The completed lines are likely to have had a greater degree of complexity than shown by de Gomme with additional palisades, lines of storm poles and a firing step for musketeers on the rampart.

The outer line diverges from the inner line near Worcester Place and follows a regimented military line around the northern suburb. The ditch has been encountered at properties on Walton Street where north-south and east–west ditches of seventeenth century date were subject to limited investigation in 2017.[46] The arrangement around the northern suburb of St Giles and its Church is poorly understood with de Gomme showing a series of defensive improvements which

---

42   Andrew Brossler, 'New University Club House Mansfield Road, Oxford', (Unpublished Oxford Archaeological Unit Report, 2003), p.4.
43   Teague, 'Balliol College Recreation Ground', p.9.
44   Humphrey Case and David Sturdy, 'Notes and News', in *Oxoniensia,* 25 (1960), p.142.
45   Kemp, *The Fortification of Oxford*, p.244.
46   Robin Bashford, 'Phase 1 Area: Somerville College, Walton Street, Oxford Archaeological Evaluation Report', (Unpublished Oxford Archaeology Report 2017); Crossley, *British Historic Towns Atlas* Map 8, Sheet N Square D8.

partially replace and partially integrate the inner line. He also shows a distinctive temporary redirection of the Banbury Road as it approached the north gate.

Further east the outer line runs through the University Science Area where the ditch has been observed multiple times. It was encountered by Cotswold Archaeology in 2015–16 during the construction of a basement for a new Physics building.[47] Here an initial ditch survived 2.25 metres wide and 50 centimetres which deep ran north-east–south-west and produced mid-seventeenth to eighteenth century pottery. A larger ditch 9.5 metres wide and 2.9 metres deep cut this feature and ran north-east–south-west then turning northwards. The later larger ditch had a steep outer northern edge and a more gently sloping inner bank with a narrow base and appeared to have been backfilled from the south where the rampart would have been located. Finds from the fill included pottery from the mid-sixteenth to seventeenth centuries, bottle glass, clay pipe and two Charles I farthings dating to 1636–1644.

In 1872 a large ditch measuring 9 metres wide and 3 metres deep was recorded at the site of the Clarendon Science Library[48] and another ditch was recorded beneath the Human Anatomy Building in 1958 which may form part of an angled bastion along the outer line.[49] Further east a 'V' shaped ditch was recorded at the Electrical Laboratory in 1909 measuring 3m metres wide and 2.5 metres deep.[50] Investigation on the site of the Geology Department Buildings in 1946 recorded a 'V' shaped ditch and a substantial bank[51] and investigations at the Pitt Rivers Museum in 2005 also recorded a substantial east–west aligned ditch approximately 6.8 metres wide and at least 1.3 metres deep of possible seventeenth century date.[52] A short distance to the east, another part of the ditch was recorded during excavations at the Department of Human Anatomy in 1959. Here, the ditch was over 8.2 metres wide with a 50 degree slope and crossed the site on a west-south-west to east-north-east alignment.[53]

47 Jonathan Hart 'Roman and Civil War Remains at the Oxford University Physics Building: Summary Report on Archaeological Investigations', in *Oxoniensia*, 84 (2019), pp.205–215.
48 HER No EOX5180; Anon 1908 Ditches under the Townsend Laboratory *Oxford Times*. Edition: 5/12/08.
49 (UAD176).
50 R.T. Lattey, et al, *A Contemporary Map of the Defences of Oxford in 1644*, p.171.
51 HER No EOX3858
52 Steve Leech, 'Land adjacent to the Pitt Rivers Museum, Oxford', Oxford Archaeology, (Unpublished report, 2005), p.6.
53 Humphrey Case and David Sturdy 1959 'Notes', in *Oxoniensia*, 24 (1959), p.101; A section of the 1959 ditch is published in Philippa Bradley and Bethan Charles et al, 'Prehistoric and Roman activity and a Civil War Ditch: Excavations at the Chemistry Research Laboratory, 2–4 South Parks Road, Oxford' in *Oxoniensia*, 70 (2005), pp.141–202; Fig 6.

The outer ditch was comprehensively revealed in plan and sectioned to the east during excavations for the Chemistry Laboratory in 2001 where it was found to be 11 metres wide and 2.4 metres deep with a profile that was broadly 45 degree slopes with a flat bottom. Here the excavator noted evidence for a shallow re-excavation along the base of the ditch which was interpreted as the later removal of a wooden defensive structure. Environmental samples from the base of the ditch produced evidence for celery leaved crowfoot and fool's watercress suggesting the presence of water or muddy conditions. The interpretation of the ditch fills suggested episodic infilling took place after the war rather than one single decisive backfilling episode.[54]

Moving eastwards the line of the ditch was identified during an extension to the Tinbergen Building in 2016, this exposed 8 metres of north-south ditch which was 4 metres wide and examined to one metre depth. This section of ditch is thought to form part of a bastion. It had a curving edge and rounded base.[55] To the east of the ditch a series of five neatly spaced steep sided rounded pits were recorded, which have been interpreted as pit falls or man traps. The pits were 2 metres in diameter and 1 metre deep; although the excavator suggested that they are likely to have been truncated by later land use. A rose farthing of Charles I (minted 1636-c.1644) was recovered from one of the pits which had stake holes in the bottom and were deliberately backfilled in one episode. One pit contained the torso of a horse, interpreted as an opportunistic disposal. Such pitfalls are described in a survey of the defences by Fairfax's council of war and in a contemporary description of the defences of Newark-on-Trent.[56] To date these are the only likely pit falls recorded by excavation in Oxford and it may be that such structures were only added around bastions rather than forming a continuous defensive line. Subsequent investigations to the south of the Tinbergen Building involved shallow trenching and an augers survey further tracked the line of the outer ditch.[57] The investigation established by shallow trenching and augering suggest that the ditch survived at 4.50m wide and to a depth of 1.80 metres.

---

54 Bradley et al, 'Prehistoric and Roman activity and a Civil War Ditch', pp.141–202.
55 Andrew Simmonds et al, *op. cit.*
56 Simmonds et al, 'Roman Settlement and the North-Eastern Civil War Defences of Oxford', p.441.
57 Andrew Simmonds, Ben M Ford and Adam Fellingham, 'Civil War Defences at the Life and Mind Building and Oxford University Sports Club Playing Field,, South Parks Road' (Oxford: Publication Report. Draft Report, 2023).

The Eastern Defences

The earthworks that survived to be illustrated on the 1st edition Ordnance Survey map on the north-eastern part of the defensive circuit do not neatly correspond to de Gomme's plan and appear to show two divergent 'outer' lines north of the original inner line that linked to Magdalen College's walled precinct. The most northern line includes a large bastion which was partly exposed in plan during a watching brief at New College Sports Ground.[58] A further earthwork that may have formed part of the defences is a shallow bank or causeway that runs north-east–south-west through the grounds of St Catherine's College, east of the River Cherwell. The bank has a ditch on its southern side so was not a defended position but may have been used to control water or as an access causeway or alternately may pre or post-date the Civil War, de Gomme shows it as a water channel.[59]

The second 'outer' line on the north-east side of the city more closely encloses the suburb of Holywell. Of this the RCHME notes that in the 1930s traces of earthwork survived behind 'a house in Manor Road' and under the Officer Training Corps building.[60] Further south this line has been investigated by Wessex Archaeology in 2012 near Manor Place, in what was formerly Holywell Mill Meadow.[61] An evaluation trench located the western terminal of ditch, which reads on Loggan's map as a water channel leading off the River Cherwell to the east. This was 10 metres wide and 3.3 metres deep. The ditch was located directly to the north of a raised natural gravel ridge, immediately to the south of which was the truncated remains of a substantial earthwork rampart measuring over 8metres wide at the base. The truncated rampart survived to a height of 700mm and was made of neat tips of re-deposited gravel and earth with a vertical interface to the north suggesting the presence of some form of revetment or gabion. The presence of a terminal to the ditch could suggest the presence of a sally port which would make more sense of the additional reinforcement in this location.

East of the River Cherwell the de Gomme map shows a defensive rampart placed around Holywell Mill, aligning with the earthworks at Manor Place. Investigations east of the mill site in 1993 revealed a curving ditch, some 4 metres wide and 1.5 metres deep, cut into the alluvium and backfilled with seventeenth century material; however the location of this feature does not closely align with this map

---

58 John Dalton 1999: 'A New College Sports Ground St Cross Road, Oxford Archaeological Watching Brief Report' (Unpublished Oxford Archaeological Unit Report).
59 Crossley, *British Historic Towns Atlas*, Plan 8, Sheet N J8.
60 RCHME 1939, p.161.
61 P. A. Harding and A. D. Crockett, 'Land at Manor Place, Oxford Archaeological Evaluation Report', (Unpublished Wessex Archaeology Report, 2012)

evidence.[62] One possibility is that this feature relates to an earlier defensive phase as the protection of the mill would have been an early concern. Further south a bastion or enclosure is shown in the Water Walks east of Magdalen College precinct and the western Cherwell channel. No archaeological investigations have taken place on these works.

The Suburb of St Clements

The de Gomme map shows a neat defensive arrangement around the medieval suburb of St Clement's on the east bank of the Cherwell, comprising a large hornwork, or starwork, with flanking bastions. According to the *Royalist Ordnance Papers* a large bridgehead work around St Clement's was started in April 1643 and armed by June.[63] Further clearance work of trees and buildings is recorded to create a field of fire eastwards.

In 1958 Oxford University Archaeological Society excavated the remains of an earth mound at Magdalen College School which was identified as Civil War in date, likely to be part of the southern bastion of the hornwork.[64] The report notes that, 'the mound, was more pronounced thirty years ago…the owners frequently found old bullets there.' It was found to consist of 'tips of gravel, loam and Oxford clay'. An east–west ditch located just to the south was identified as of Civil War date. The mound is still visible as a very slight rise and may relate to one of the horn work bastions shown by de Gomme.[65]

Small scale investigations have located three further sizeable ditches backfilled with seventeenth century material in St Clement's, none of which neatly conform to the de Gomme line. At numbers 31–34 St Clements, a substantial, undated, ditch was identified beneath a nineteenth century cellar.[66] In 1983, approximately 60 metres to the west, another poorly dated substantial ditch was recorded as 17 metres wide and 3.5 metres deep.[67] In 2006 excavations some 60 metres outside the projected route of the starwork, to the south of Magdalen College School, recorded

---

62   Chris Bell, 'Holywell Ford Oxford Archaeological Evaluation', (Unpublished Oxford Archaeological Unit Report, 1993)
63   *ROP*, 469.
64   Humphrey Case 'Archaeological Notes', in *Oxoniensia*, 23 (1958), p.136.
65   Crossley, *British Historic Towns Atlas*, Map 8 Sheet N K3&4.
66   Brian Durham, 'OXFORD: 31-34 St. Clements', in *South Midlands Archaeology*, CBA Group 9 Newsletter. Edition: 11, 1981: p.133.
67   HER EOX4880; *Oxford Archaeological Unit Notebooks* Edition 6, 1981–83.

a north-north-east to south-south-west aligned ditch approximately 4.5 metres wide containing seventeenth century material.[68]

Section by the Physic Garden

South of Bridge Street (now High Street) a small section of earthwork was built as part of a defence of the west bank of the Magdalen Bridge crossing, linking to the walled precinct of the Physic Garden, later the Botanical garden, which had been constructed in the 1620s. A work from Magdalen bridge to the corner of the walled garden is mentioned above. Anthony Wood describes the construction of a further section of defences linking the south western corner of the garden with the corner of Merton College and the city wall.

The Southern and Western Defences

The defences of the south-east quadrant of the city were designed to protect the southern suburb of St Aldate's and create a field of fire over the expansive Christ Church Meadow which could be partly flooded by damming various channels. A line of earthworks, broken by staggered obtuse changes in alignment, is shown by de Gomme protecting the city wall and creating flanking firing positions of simple character, similar to the inner line to the north. These may be the 1643 works referenced in the *Royalist Ordnance Papers* in the meadows and at Folly Bridge.

More precisely drawn bastions are shown as this line turns south along the approximate route of the New Walk through Christ Church Meadow to protect the southern suburb of St Aldate's. A second, and presumed later, east–west outer line crosses through the meadow south of Merton Field and a large defence bastion known as 'Half-Moon' or 'Dunsmore' Sconce straddles the meeting point of the Trill Mill Stream and a branch of the River Cherwell, creating an odd defensive feature if built as shown. Munby suggests that the channels enclosed by the firing position here may have been temporarily diverted to flood the meadow and would otherwise have been dry.[69]

In 2014 a trial trench excavated east of the nineteenth century thatched barn in the western part of Christ Church Meadow recorded a compacted platform of limestone rubble. The platform was not closely dated although post-medieval pottery, consistent with a Civil War date for the feature, was found on the platform

---

68   Robin Bashford, 'Magdalen College School: Archaeological Evaluation Report', (Unpublished Oxford Archaeology Report, 2006), p.4.
69   Munby, 'Note on Oxford's Civil War Earthworks', p56.

surface and the feature could relate to the north-south Royalist line running parallel to St Aldate's, potentially forming a firing platform.[70]

In the south-west quadrant the de Gomme map shows a defensive line encompassing three very large bastions in the fashion of the 'half-moon sconce' linked by a continuous rampart and with enclosures protecting the southern approach via Folly Bridge and enclosing St Thomas' Church and the parish of that name. West of the Castle Mill Stream the defences follow a very similar line to drainage ditches shown on post-medieval and later maps before encircling St Thomas's Church.[71]

De Gomme shows these south-west quadrant defences as dotted lines and a corrective piece of paper has been placed over the line leading to some uncertainty about whether the line was built in this area. The Westgate excavation in 2015–16 provided an opportunity to examine the projected line and confirmed its presence. The defences were revealed in plan and four sections were excavated showing a more rectangular defensive formation than the neat arrangement shown by de Gomme. The bastion line appears to have pragmatically adapted to existing landscape features in this case sluices and a channel coming off the Trill Mill Stream to the north.[72] The ditch of the bastion had a concave profile, the widest profiles measured 6.4 metres across and the deepest recorded section was 1.46 metres. The lower fills comprised blue-grey clay/silts or rich black organic deposits, suggesting that they held standing water at some stage before being deliberately backfilled in the late seventeenth or early eighteenth century.

At the southern tip of the defensive line, west of Folly Bridge, a further defensive outer line is shown by de Gomme, this has never been investigated. A further amorphous and curving outer ditch is shown further west on Taylor's 1750 map mirroring the north bank of the Thames and is marked 'remains of the trenches' but the date and character of any earthworks here are unknown.

From the Church of St Thomas the rampart ran north joining the moat around the remnants of Rewley Abbey, which at this time retained its stone, precinct wall. This line was investigated during a watching brief south of the former LMS station prior to the construction of the Said Business School in 1999.[73] Here 20 metres of the defensive line were exposed in plan. The ditch was seen to be 12 metres wide and was only excavated to a depth of 1 metre. A distinctive feature was a 2.5 metres wide berm that separated the ditch from the truncated remains of a rampart to

---

70 Graham Keevill and Kathy Keevill, 'Christ Church, Oxford: The Thatched Barn Archaeological Evaluation Report', (Unpublished Keevill Heritage Ltd Report, 2014), p.19.
71 Crossley, *British Historic Towns Atlas,* Map 8 Sheet N C4 and D4.
72 Steve Teague, 'Westgate Centre, Oxford Post-Excavation Assessment and Updated Project Design', (Unpublished Oxford Archaeology Report, 2019)
73 Julian Munby et al, *From Studium to Station,* p.31.

the east. The rampart bank was made of tips of gravel and earth and survived to a depth of 500mm and was 8 metres wide. A deposit of limestone rubble, some of it worked, lay on the berm, and the excavator suggested this may have been used to revet the face of the rampart.

Forts and Sconces

Beyond the defensive circuit de Gomme shows a number of outer defensive positions. To the east an outlying fortlet firing position was placed within the grounds of Magdalen College and described as 'Dover's Speare', here a rectilinear arrangement of drainage channels survives which appear to be in part the recut ditches of the earthwork.

To the south of the Thames crossing, a star work is shown surrounding Eastwyke Farm on the Abingdon Road. The surviving earthworks here were plotted in 2010;[74] a sub rectilinear moat or drainage ditch survives around the early seventeenth century Eastwyke Cottage, although the earthwork is believed to predate the siege.[75] Further west at Oxpens Meadow 'Hart's Sconce' is marked occupying an island in the Thames Channels. The site has been recently subject to geophysical survey, which produced a faint reading in the rough shape of the sconce. A section through the projected ditch did not recover a clear ditch profile, however an extensive area covered by several layers containing seventeenth century finds along with two steep sided pits, a stakehole and a shallow pit or ditch were noted. It is possible the shallow pit is the remains of the northern part of the sconce ditch.[76]

West of the city a small square sconce or fortlet is shown defending the powder mill at Osney, and a map of 1829 shows ditches belonging to this.[77] The multi-period fabric of the standing mill was surveyed in 2008 and found to contain medieval and post-medieval fabric.[78] The site of the fortlet to the west lies below the current Lock Keeper's cottage. Further north another similar fort or sconce is shown just beyond the walled precinct at Rewley Abbey. A trench in this location in 1994 recorded a 5 metre wide ditch excavated to only 50cm because of the high

---

74 Laura Gadsby, 'Eastwyke Farmhouse, Abingdon Road, Oxford. Earthwork Survey'. (Unpublished Cotswold Archaeology Report, 2010).
75 https://historicengland.org.uk/listing/the-list/list-entry/1369700?section=official-list-entry.
76 Kirsty Smith and Elizabeth Stafford, 'Oxpens Oxford Masterplan including enabling works area Archaeological Evaluation Report', (Unpublished Oxford Archaeology Report, 2023)
77 Osney Cart II, p.627 – the map records 'sconce' field here.
78 Simon Underdown, 'Osney Mill, Oxford, Historic Building Recording and Investigation' (Unpublished Oxford Archaeology Report, 2015).

water table. Rough limestone pieces which ran along the north side of ditch may have revetted a bank, perhaps part of the fort.[79]

Parliamentarian Positions

De Gomme shows the Parliamentary lines on Headington Hill, however attempts to locate the Parliamentarian line in South Parks using geophysical survey have been unsuccessful.[80] A visible break in slope in South Parks is an obvious location for Parliamentary positions. The first positive identification of the Parliamentarian line at Headington Hill comes via the examination of Lidar information in 2022 by Sam Wilson, who has identified a small square fortlet with lines running off in Headington Hill Park that is relatable to the positions mapped by de Gomme.[81]

To the north of Oxford at Port Meadow at least two 'V' shaped gun positions that face towards the city are recorded on an 1827 map and one remains partly visible in wet conditions.[82] These earthworks have been suggested to be part of a scheme to allow the control of flooding to make the meadow impassable.[83] A further rectilinear earthwork adjoining a shallow north-south bank located south of Osney Mead could potentially be part of a siege position.[84]

Outlying Positions

The stone walled precincts of Littlemore Priory, Godstow Abbey and Bartlemas Leper Hospital were all utilised during the Civil War and investigations in each have revealed a background noise of Civil War activity. These and other Civil War activity beyond the immediate siegeworks and defences are outside the scope of this paper.

---

79   Julian Munby, Andy Simmonds, Ric Tyler and David R P Wilkinson, *From Studium to Station Rewley Abbey and Rewley Road Station, Oxford*, (Oxford: Oxford Archaeology Occasional Paper Number 16, 2007), pp.31–32.
80   Olaf Bayer, 'South Park: Interpretation of Earthworks' in David Griffiths and Jane Harrison, *The Archaeology of East Oxford Archeox: the Development of a Community* (Thames Valley Landscapes Monograph 43, Oxford University Department for Continuing Education, 2020), pp.98–103.
81   Pers. Comm. Sam Wilson.
82   St John's Coll. Mun., Map 42; D Sturdy *op. cit.,* 136–7, Fig 3.
83   Rebecca Briscoe, *The Archaeological Potential for LiDAR Survey in the Thames Floodplain Port Meadow and its Environs*, p.5 fig. 2 and p.30 plate 5 (unpublished report, 2006); Munby 'Note on Oxford's Civil War Earthworks', p.56.
84   Pers. Comm. Sam Wilson.

Discussion

Contrary to the comments of Kemp who suggested that, 'archaeological excavation would hardly be profitable… all that would be discovered would probably be a few cannon balls and musket shot,'[85] archaeological investigation has proved effective at gradually enabling the reconstruction the Royalist capital's defences. We can see how the defensive lines initially compromised military symmetry for the expediency of using existing landscape features, how ditches were profiled and recut, how different work parties constructed different parts of the defensive ramparts and fortified outer positions with palisades and pit falls. The recorded profiles and dimensions seem to vary considerably, taking into account the likely varying degrees of truncation, suggesting piecemeal and hurried construction.

Although the creation of a 'line with redoubts and a foot-place' was being discussed in August 1642[86] it remains unproved whether this was ever substantively initiated before Parliamentarian troops entered the city in September and orders were given to slight the defensive works. It is unclear if the University Chancellor and his adviser Sir Richard Cave had the tools, manpower, time or discipline to construct anything substantial in the short window of time available. Wood records that Lord Saye, the newly appointed Lord Lieutenant of Oxfordshire, gave the order that the 'works and trenches that the scholars had made across the highways about the town' should be removed which reads more of a removal of localised obstructions near to access routes rather than the large-scale slighting of a long defensive work constructed between the two rivers.[87] The local MP who ridiculed the scholars for working 'night and day with mattocks and shovels' could have been referring to much more modest trenching near the main access roads.[88] However, if the University was not responsible for the establishment of the inner line it raises the question as to why such an *ad hoc* series of defensive alignments was subsequently established given the military expertise available.

Archaeological investigations have shown that while de Gomme's map is largely accurate there are significant variations in the line and character of the fortifications. It is likely that further complexities remain to be discovered. What is clear is that the disciplined symmetry of Rawlinson's initial defensive plan was quickly jettisoned of more pragmatic considerations. Eventually military discipline prevailed and a more militarily robust outer line was established. Ultimately the

---

85   Kemp, *The Fortification of Oxford*, p.245.
86   HMC. Portland Mss I.59
87   Wood, *Life and Times,* p.61.
88   H.M.C. Portland MSS., I, 59.

defences were sufficient to deter direct Parliamentarian assault and the lines were never tested by serious military engagement.[89]

Bibliography

Contemporary Documents
Calendar of State Papers Domestic Series
H.M.C. Portland Mss. I.
The Oseney Cartulary. Vol. II: 90 (Oxford: Oxford Historical Society First Series, 1928)
Ian Roy, *The Royalist Ordnance Papers*, (Oxford: Oxfordshire Records Society 1964 & 1975)
St John's College, Oxford. Mun. Map 42

Published
Barratt John, *Cavalier Capital: Oxford in the English Civil War 1642-1646* (Solihull: Helion & Company Ltd, 2015)
Bell, Chris, 'Archaeological Investigations on the site of a medieval and post-medieval watermill at Holywell Ford, Magdalen College, Oxford', in *Oxoniensia*, 61, 1996, pp.275–96
Bradley, Philippa et al, 2005 'Prehistoric and Roman activity and a Civil War Ditch: Excavations at the Chemistry Research Laboratory, 2-4 South Parks Road, Oxford', in *Oxoniensia*, 70, 2005, pp.141–202
Case, Humphrey, 1958 'Archaeological Notes', in *Oxoniensia,* 23, 1958, 130–8
Crossley, Allan (ed.), *British Historic Towns Atlas Volume VII Oxford Introduction and Gazetteer* (The Historic Town Trust, 2021)
Durham, Brian et al, Oxford's Northern Defences: Archaeological Studies 1971–1982, in *Oxoniensia*, 48, 1983, pp.13—40
Hart, Jonathan, 'Roman and Civil War Remains at the Oxford University Physics Building: Summary Report on Archaeological Investigations', in *Oxoniensia* 84, 2019, pp.205–215
Kemp, Anthony, 'The Fortification of Oxford during the Civil War' in *Oxoniensia, 42, 1977, pp.237-246*
Lattey, R.T. et al, 'A Contemporary Map of the Defences of Oxford in 1644', in *Oxoniensia*, 1, 1936, pp.161–172
Madan, J. A., *Catalogue of Oxford Books* (Oxford: Clarendon Press, 1912)

---

[89] In fact the city suffered far greater damage from a fire started accidentally by Royalist soldiers in October 1644; J. Barratt, *Cavalier Capital Oxford in the Civil War 1642–1646*, p.145.

Munby, Julian, et al, *Excavations at Oxford Castle 1999–2009* (York: Thames Valley Landscapes Monograph, No 44, 2019)

Munby, Julian et al, *From Studium to Station Rewley Abbey and Rewley Road Station, Oxford* (Oxford: Oxford Archaeology Occasional Paper No 16, 2007)

RCHM 1939: An Inventory of the Historical Monuments in the City of Oxford, (London, Royal Commission on Historical Monuments, 1939)

Ian Roy and Dietrich Reinhart 'Oxford and the Civil Wars' in Nicholas Tyacke (ed.) *The History of the University of Oxford: Volume IV Seventeenth Century* (Oxford: OUP, 1997)

Saunders, Andrew, *Fortress Builder. Bernard de Gomme, Charles II's Military Engineer* (Exeter: University of Exeter Press, 2004)

Simmons, Andrew, et al, 'Roman Settlement and the North-Eastern Civil War Defences of Oxford: Investigations at Mansfield College and the Tinbergen Building' in Dodd, A, et al (eds), *The Archaeology of Oxford in the 21st Century, Investigations in the City by Oxford Archaeology, 2006–16* (Oxford: OAHS Occasional Paper **1,** 2020)

Simmonds, Andrew et al, 'A Seventeenth Century Burial and Medieval to Post-Medieval Tenement Plots at St Cross College', in Dodd, A, et al (eds) *The Archaeology of Oxford in the 21st Century, Investigations in the City by Oxford Archaeology, 2006–16* (Oxford: OAHS Occasional Paper 1, 2020)

Sturdy, David, *Historic Oxford* (Stroud: Tempus, 2004)

Varley, Frederick J., *The Siege of Oxford: An Account of Oxford During the Civil War, 1642–1646* (Oxford: OUP, 1932)

Varley, Frederick J., *Supplement to the Siege of Oxford* (Oxford: OUP, 1935)

Unpublished

Bashford, Robin, *Magdalen College School: Archaeological Evaluation Report* (Unpublished Oxford Archaeology Report, 2006)

Bashford, Robin, *Exeter College, Ruskin Building, Walton Street, Oxford Archaeological Watching Brief Report*, (Unpublished Oxford Archaeology Report, 2015)

Bashford, Robin, *New College, Longwall Street, Archaeological Evaluation* (Unpublished Oxford Archaeology Report, 2015)

Bashford, Robin *Phase 1 Area: Somerville College, Walton Street, Oxford Archaeological Evaluation Report* (Unpublished Oxford Archaeology Report 2017)

Bell, Chris, 1993 *New College Mound, An Investigation* (Oxford Archaeological Unit Unpublished Report, 1993)

Harding, Phillip. A. & Crockett, Andy. D., *Land at Manor Place, Oxford Archaeological Evaluation Report* (Unpublished Wessex Archaeology Report No. 87340, 2012)

Imogen Grundon, *An archaeological watching brief at the site of the old LMS Station* (AOC Archaeological Group Unpublished Report, 1999)

Keevill, Graham and Keevill Cathy, *Christ Church, Oxford: The Thatched Barn, Archaeological Evaluation Report* (Unpublished Keevill Heritage Ltd Report, 2014)

Simmonds, Andrew and Martin, T., *Love Lane Building Mansfield College* (Unpublished Oxford Archaeological Excavation Report, 2017)

Smith, K. & Stafford, E., *Oxpens, Oxford (Masterplan, including Enabling Works Area) Archaeological Evaluation Report* (Unpublished Oxford Archaeology Report 2023)

Teague, Steve *Westgate Centre, Oxford Post-Excavation Assessment and Updated Project Design Volume 1: Main Text* (Unpublished Oxford Archaeology Report 2019)

Underdown, Simon, *Osney Mill Oxford Historic Building Recording and Investigation* (Unpublished Oxford Archaeology Report, 2015)

Other titles in the Century of the Soldier series

No 1 *'Famous by my Sword'*: The Army of Montrose and the Military Revolution

No 2 *Marlborough's Other Army*: The British Army and the Campaigns of the First Peninsular War, 1702–1712

No 3 *Cavalier Capital*: Oxford in the English Civil War 1642–1646

No 4 *Reconstructing the New Model Army*: Vol 1: Regimental Lists April 1645 to May 1649

No 5 *To Settle the Crown*: Waging Civil War in Shropshire, 1642–1648

No 6 *The First British Army, 1624–1628*: The Army of the Duke of Buckingham

No 7 *Better Begging Than Fighting*: The Royalist Army in Exile in the War against Cromwell 1656–1660

No 8 *Reconstructing the New Model Army*: Vol 2: Regimental Lists April 1649 to May 1663

No 9 *The Battle of Montgomery 1644*: The English Civil War in the Welsh Borderlands

No 10 *The Arte Militaire*: The Application of 17th Century Military Manuals to Conflict Archaeology

No 11 *No Armour But Courage*: Colonel Sir George Lisle, 1615–1648

No 12 *Cromwell's Buffoon*: The Life and Career of the Regicide, Thomas Pride

No 14 *Hey for Old Robin!* The Campaigns and Armies of the Earl of Essex During the First Civil War, 1642–44

No 15 *The Bavarian Army during the Thirty Years War*

No 16 *The Army of James II, 1685-1688*: The Birth of the British Army

No 17 *Civil War London*: A Military History of London under Charles I and Oliver Cromwell

No 18 *The Other Norfolk Admirals*: Myngs, Narbrough and Shovell

No 19 *A New Way of Fighting*: Professionalism in the English Civil War

No 20 *Crucible of the Jacobite '15*: The Battle of Sheriffmuir 1715

No 21 *'A Rabble of Gentility'*: The Royalist Northern Horse, 1644–45

No 22 *Peter the Great Humbled*: The Russo-Ottoman War of 1711

No 23 *The Russian Army In The Great Northern War 1700–21*: Organisation, Matériel, Training, Combat Experience and Uniforms

No 24 *The Last Army*: The Battle of Stow-on-the-Wold and the End of the Civil War in the Welsh Marches, 1646

No 25 *The Battle of the White Mountain 1620 and the Bohemian Revolt, 1618–22*

No 26 *The Swedish Army in the Great Northern War 1700–21*: Organisation, Equipment, Campaigns and Uniforms

No 27 *St. Ruth's Fatal Gamble*: The Battle of Aughrim 1691 and the Fall Of Jacobite Ireland

No 28 *Muscovy's Soldiers*: The Emergence of the Russian Army 1462–1689

No 29 *Home and Away*: The British Experience of War 1618–1721

No 30 *From Solebay to the Texel*: The Third Anglo-Dutch War, 1672–1674

No 31 *The Battle of Killiecrankie*: The First Jacobite Campaign, 1689–1691

No 32 *The Most Heavy Stroke*: The Battle of Roundway Down 1643

No 33 *The Cretan War (1645–1671)*: The Venetian-Ottoman Struggle in the Mediterranean

No 34 *Peter the Great's Revenge*: The Russian Siege of Narva in 1704

No 35 *The Battle Of Glenshiel*: The Jacobite Rising in 1719

No 36 *Armies And Enemies Of Louis XIV*: Volume 1 - Western Europe 1688–1714: France, Britain, Holland

No 37 *William III's Italian Ally*: Piedmont and the War of the League of Augsburg 1683–1697

No 38 *Wars and Soldiers in the Early Reign of Louis XIV*: Volume 1 - The Army of the United Provinces of the Netherlands, 1660–1687

No 39 *In The Emperor's Service*: Wallenstein's Army, 1625–1634

No 40 *Charles XI's War*: The Scanian War Between Sweden and Denmark, 1675–1679

No 41 *The Armies and Wars of The Sun King 1643–1715*: Volume 1: The Guard of Louis XIV

No 42 *The Armies Of Philip IV Of Spain 1621–1665*: The Fight For European Supremacy

No 43 *Marlborough's Other Army*: The British Army and the Campaigns of the First Peninsular War, 1702–1712

No 44 *The Last Spanish Armada*: Britain And The War Of The Quadruple Alliance, 1718–1720

No 45 *Essential Agony*: The Battle of Dunbar 1650

No 46 *The Campaigns of Sir William Waller*

No 47 *Wars and Soldiers in the Early Reign of Louis XIV*: Volume 2 - The Imperial Army, 1660–1689

No 48 *The Saxon Mars and His Force*: The Saxon Army During The Reign Of John George III 1680–1691

No 49 *The King's Irish*: The Royalist Anglo-Irish Foot of the English Civil War

No 50 *The Armies and Wars of the Sun King 1643–1715*: Volume 2: The Infantry of Louis XIV

No 51 *More Like Lions Than Men*: Sir William Brereton and the Cheshire Army of Parliament, 1642–46

No 52 *I Am Minded to Rise*: The Clothing, Weapons and Accoutrements of the Jacobites from 1689 to 1719

No 53 *The Perfection of Military Discipline*: The Plug Bayonet and the English Army 1660–1705

No 54 *The Lion From the North*: The Swedish Army During the Thirty Years War: Volume 1, 1618–1632

No 55 *Wars and Soldiers in the Early Reign of Louis XIV*: Volume 3 - The Armies of the Ottoman Empire 1645–1718

No 56 *St. Ruth's Fatal Gamble*: The Battle of Aughrim 1691 and the Fall Of Jacobite Ireland

No 57 *Fighting for Liberty*: Argyll & Monmouth's Military Campaigns against the Government of King James, 1685

No 58 *The Armies and Wars of the Sun King 1643–1715*: Volume 3: The Cavalry of Louis XIV

No 59 *The Lion From the North*: The Swedish Army During the Thirty Years War: Volume 2, 1632–1648

No 60 *By Defeating My Enemies*: Charles XII of Sweden and the Great Northern War 1682–1721

No 61 *Despite Destruction, Misery and Privations..*: The Polish Army in Prussia during the war against Sweden 1626–1629

No 62 *The Armies of Sir Ralph Hopton*: The Royalist Armies of the West 1642–46

No 63 *Italy, Piedmont, and the War of the Spanish Succession 1701–1712*

No 64 *'Cannon played from the great fort'*: Sieges in the Severn Valley during the English Civil War 1642–1646

No 65 *Carl Gustav Armfelt and the Struggle for Finland During the Great Northern War*

No 66 *In the Midst of the Kingdom*: The Royalist War Effort in the North Midlands 1642–1646

No 67 *The Anglo-Spanish War 1655-1660*: Volume 1: The War in the West Indies

No 68 *For a Parliament Freely Chosen*: The Rebellion of Sir George Booth, 1659

No 69 *The Bavarian Army During the Thirty Years War 1618–1648*: The Backbone of the Catholic League (revised second edition)

No 70 *The Armies and Wars of the Sun King 1643–1715*: Volume 4: The War of the Spanish Succession, Artillery, Engineers and Militias

No 71 *No Armour But Courage*: Colonel Sir George Lisle, 1615–1648 (Paperback reprint)

No 72 **The New Knights:** The Development of Cavalry in Western Europe, 1562–1700

No 73 **Cavalier Capital:** Oxford in the English Civil War 1642–1646 (Paperback reprint)

No 74 **The Anglo-Spanish War 1655–1660:** Volume 2: War in Jamaica

No 75 **The Perfect Militia:** The Stuart Trained Bands of England and Wales 1603–1642

No 76 **Wars and Soldiers in the Early Reign of Louis XIV:** Volume 4 - The Armies of Spain 1659–1688

No 77 **The Battle of Nördlingen 1634:** The Bloody Fight Between Tercios and Brigades

No 78 **Wars and Soldiers in the Early Reign of Louis XIV:** Volume 5 - The Portuguese Army 1659–1690

No 79 **We Came, We Saw, God Conquered:** The Polish-Lithuanian Commonwealth's military effort in the relief of Vienna, 1683

No 80 **Charles X's Wars:** Volume 1 - Armies of the Swedish Deluge, 1655–1660

No 81 **Cromwell's Buffoon:** The Life and Career of the Regicide, Thomas Pride (Paperback reprint)

No 82 **The Colonial Ironsides:** English Expeditions under the Commonwealth and Protectorate, 1650–1660

No 83 **The English Garrison of Tangier:** Charles II's Colonial Venture in the Mediterranean, 1661–1684

No 84 **The Second Battle of Preston, 1715:** The Last Battle on English Soil

No 85 **To Settle the Crown:** Waging Civil War in Shropshire, 1642–1648 (Paperback reprint)

No 86 **A Very Gallant Gentleman:** Colonel Francis Thornhagh (1617–1648) and the Nottinghamshire Horse

No 87 **Charles X's Wars:** Volume 2 - The Wars in the East, 1655–1657

No 88 **The Shōgun's Soldiers:** The Daily Life of Samurai and Soldiers in Edo Period Japan, 1603–1721 Volume 1

No 89 **Campaigns of the Eastern Association:** The Rise of Oliver Cromwell, 1642–1645

No 90 **The Army of Occupation in Ireland 1603–42:** Defending the Protestant Hegemony

No 91 **The Armies and Wars of the Sun King 1643–1715:** Volume 5: Buccaneers and Soldiers in the Americas

No 92 **New Worlds, Old Wars:** The Anglo-American Indian Wars 1607–1678

No 93 **Against the Deluge:** Polish and Lithuanian Armies During the War Against Sweden 1655–1660

No 94 **The Battle of Rocroi:** The Battle, the Myth and the Success of Propaganda

No 95 **The Shōgun's Soldiers:** The Daily Life of Samurai and Soldiers in Edo Period Japan, 1603–1721 Volume 2

No 96 **Science of Arms: the Art of War in the Century of the Soldier 1672–1699:** Volume 1: Preparation for War and the Infantry

No 97 **Charles X's Wars:** Volume 3 - The Danish Wars 1657–1660

No 98 **Wars and Soldiers in the Early Reign of Louis XIV:** Volume 6 - Armies of the Italian States 1660–1690 Part 1

No 99 **Dragoons and Dragoon Operations in the British Civil Wars, 1638–1653**

No 100 **Wars and Soldiers in the Early Reign of Louis XIV:** Volume 6 - Armies of the Italian States 1660–1690 Part 2

No 101 **1648 and All That:** The Scottish Invasions of England, 1648 and 1651: Proceedings of the 2022 Helion and Company 'Century of the Soldier' Conference

No 102 **John Hampden and the Battle of Chalgrove:** The Political and Military Life of Hampden and his Legacy

No 103 **The City Horse:** London's militia cavalry during the English Civil War, 1642–1660

No 104 **The Battle of Lützen 1632:** A Reassessment

No 105 **Monmouth's First Rebellion:** The Later Covenanter Risings, 1660–1685

No 106 **Raw Generals and Green Soldiers:** Catholic Armies in Ireland 1641–1643

No 107 **The Khotyn Campaign:** Polish, Lithuanian and Cossack armies versus the might of the Ottoman Empire

No 108 **Soldiers and Civilians, Transport and Provisions:** Early Modern Military Logistics and Supply Systems During The British Civil Wars, 1638-1653

No 109 **Batter their walls, gates and Forts:** The Proceedings of the 2022 English Civil War Fortress Symposium

SERIES SPECIALS:

No 1 **Charles XII's Karoliners:** Volume 1: The Swedish Infantry & Artillery of the Great Northern War 1700–1721